FLAVOUR

FLAVOUR

Everyday Food Made Exceptional

MARK MORIARTY

GILL BOOKS

Gill Books
Hume Avenue
Park West
Dublin 12
www.gillbooks.ie

Gill Books is an imprint of
M.H. Gill and Co.

978 07171 97477

Designed by Graham Thew
Edited by Wendy Hobson
Photography by Cliodhna Prendergast
Food styling by Orla Neligan
Proofread by Catherine Gough
Indexed by Eileen O'Neill
Printed and bound by L.E.G.O. SpA, Italy

This book is typeset in Elena Basic 11pt
The paper used in this book comes
from the wood pulp of sustainably
managed forests.

A CIP catalogue record for this book is
available from the British Library.

5 4 3 2

MIX
Paper | Supporting
responsible forestry
FSC® C023419

Contents

Part Four: **Longer Dishes**

Introduction

Hello, my name is Mark Moriarty and I have been mad about food and cooking for as long as I can remember.

In the pages ahead you'll find a collection of recipes that I hope will make you think five things when you read them:

1   That looks delicious, I would love to get my spoon into that and eat it right now.
2   That dish is familiar, I've made it before.
3   Those are ingredients I already have.
4   There's a handy trick I didn't know I could use.
5   I am going to give that a try.

If you thought about any of the above, then I'm on the right track, and I would love this book to be your go-to for perfecting the basics of home cooking.

These are my versions of the dishes we all know and love, many of them inspired by the meals people I have worked with have cooked through the years. I've broken the book down into moments: from smaller, lighter dishes and quick midweek ideas to blowout weekend specials, sweets and breads for when you've time to commit. I've also included my basics range: a short guide on how to cook simple things perfectly. You'd be surprised how many professional chefs even get these wrong!

As this is my first book, let me give you a short insight into who I am, and how this all came about.

I had what most would consider a fairly uneventful and normal upbringing, if there is such a thing! My parents, Monica and Tom, were both involved in mental health services and worked extremely long hours. They placed great emphasis on sitting down every night as a family, with my sister Laura and me, to eat dinner. This made food a central part of growing up. Now he won't mind me saying this, but Tom wasn't great at cooking. In fairness, he is getting better since retiring but I still question his attitude and patience. Monica was the star of our kitchen and, in hindsight, we ate like royalty most nights. Lasagnes, chicken and broccoli bakes, stir-fries and, if we behaved, a few Thursday night fairy cakes! As I get older, I really start to marvel at how she made it all happen day in, day out with so many commitments. She was, and is to this day, an inspiration. My nana, Ena, was the same, and used to go out of her way to bring me to Howth to buy fish for fish and chips. Richie would make the brown bread and chips to go alongside. Special memories to have. I've also been told that I used to rate visits to my friends' houses based on what their parents would make for dinner. What a little s**t! Thankfully I still have a few friends left. Andrew was best man at my wedding and his mother, Marie, was another early inspiration. I used to come home raving about her roast potatoes and revolutionary addition of pine nuts to a salad. I've included her scone recipe in this book.

Apart from family, the second thing that shaped my early interest in food was in Ventry, County Kerry. While we lived and went to school in Dublin, any time off was spent in the far reaches of the Dingle Peninsula. My dad had, and still has, a small inshore fishing boat. In the same way that he fished with his father there growing up, we would plan each day around weather, tides and different spots all the way from the turf banks at Ventry beach to the far reaches of the outer Blasket Islands, thinking about the massive fish they could be hiding. Without realising it at the time, I was gaining an appreciation of where food comes from, the people sourcing it, and the places it represents.

The obsession with fishing soon developed into cooking the catch, practising with everything from mackerel and pollock to turbot, black sole, lobster and crab. I grew up with a generation of TV chefs and the wonders of the internet. This allowed me to soak up the passion 24/7. Hugh Fearnley-Whittingstall and his exploits at River Cottage took up most weekends; I hope to meet him some day. I could also quote every line from Heston Blumenthal's *In Search of Perfection* series. While my friends in school were hitting their first teenage discos, I was at home making hollandaise. Weekends were spent cutting recipe features out of newspapers.

I was fortunate to have a clear idea of what I wanted to do early on. When the opportunity for work experience came along in school, I spent the day writing the same letter ten times and posting it to what I thought were the ten best restaurants in Ireland at the time. I'm indebted to the three chefs who wrote back and brought a clueless 15-year-old into their kitchens for a month. When I left them, I had discovered the greatest job in the world.

My first 'real' job was in The Chart House restaurant in Dingle the following summer. I was still clueless, immature, emotional and always tired. The reality of being a chef was tough, but with the support of the owner, Jim, the patience and example from the head chef, Noel, along with some tough love from Monica and

Tom, I got through it. I didn't quit when that would have been the easiest thing to do, and I never looked back. There's a lesson in that.

Being a chef and involved in food has served me well ever since, along with a lot of good luck and fortunate timing. The perceived success I have achieved is completely a product of all the people I have worked for and with, who have always been so generous with their time and training. So far, there's been laughs and tears, awards, lists, tours around the world, TV shows, Michelin-star-winning teams, documentaries, mentors, friendships, an incredibly beautiful and supportive wife, and loads of amazing food.

And that brings us to this first book.

It doesn't matter if you're working in a Michelin-starred kitchen, cooking for a loved one at home, for yourself or for the family this weekend. Putting a smile on somebody's face with food is one of life's great joys.

I hope this book helps you make everyday food exceptional.

Mark

Cooking notes

It was important to me to make sure that this book is as user-friendly as possible in all kinds of ways.

Ingredients

Maybe it's just me, but I get frustrated reading through recipes with bespoke ingredients from far-flung corners of the world. Yes, I would love to be authentic 100% of the time, but it's not always possible on a Tuesday night after a 12-hour shift! For the most part, these recipes contain ingredients you might already have in your fridge or cupboard.

Oil wise, I stick with vegetable or sunflower oil if I'm heating it. Generally, the better the quality of oil, the less you should be cooking with it. I keep quality olive oils for drizzling at the end, almost as an extra layer of seasoning. If olive oil heats up, the flavour enzymes break down, a bitter taste appears, the colour bleaches and it loses all the goodness.

You'll also notice I use a small pool of store cupboard staples for adjusting the seasoning in different recipes: soy sauce, Dijon mustard, Worcestershire sauce, stockpots, tabasco. In the restaurant we called these 'jiggy bits' and they are a handy way to make good food great. When we don't have hours to develop layers of flavour in food, these ingredients help deliver a punch with the drop of a spoon. Use them sparingly and notice the difference, and rest assured that top chefs around the world are often doing the same with their home cooking.

Weighing and measuring

To make them quick and convenient to prepare, I've tried to avoid weighing ingredients for savoury dishes, so you'll see tablespoons and teaspoons in place of grams. There are specific weights for meat and fish, but you can ask the butcher or fishmonger to weigh them for you. Where I'm using ingredients like mince, chicken breasts or tinned tomatoes, I've tried to keep the quantities similar to the amount you get in your average packet or tin so it's already weighed for you. That only leaves you to get out the scales for the sweet recipes and that's unavoidable, I'm afraid, as they are an exact science!

Equipment

Equipment wise, I have very little at home and this is reflected in the recipes. If you do want to invest in some kit to make your life easier, I'd recommend the following:

- NON-STICK PAN Wash it by hand with a soft cloth after every use and it will last for ever.
- CASSEROLE DISH I use one large flameproof and ovenproof casserole dish for slow cooking everything.
- KNIVES I use a quality 25cm chef's knife that I sharpen with a stone regularly (you can YouTube how) and a cheap small paring knife. That's it, all you need.
- HOME BLENDER I use a nutribullet-style blender, a fantastic investment that saves me loads of time when I'm cooking at home.
- MIXER I use a Kenwood mixer with a whisk and dough hook attachment. This is ideal for most of the sweet recipes and breads in the book and saves a lot of energy making things by hand.
- STEAMER This is essential for making my Perfectly cooked rice (page 15).

Quantities

During the week, I like to bulk up some of these recipes if I have time. I keep a selection of airtight plastic containers so I can easily pack and store the extras in the fridge and freezer. This means I can pull something out on the days I just can't be bothered to cook. The recipes will still work if you double up from two to four or even four to eight, while giving you the chance to stock up – just like a professional kitchen.

Ireland's finest

Finally, yes, I use a lot of butter. It's one of Ireland's world-class ingredients. I tend to use salted butter – except for the Sticky toffee pudding (page 170) – but both are superb so you can make your own choices.

As a chef, I'm also pretty liberal with my use of salt and lemon juice. If you don't want to add as much, you don't have to!

Part One: The Basics

Like most things in life, success relies on doing the basics right. How many times have we heard that in a sports report or a team meeting at work? Cooking is no different. These may seem like very simple recipes, but I've included a few tips and tricks to ensure perfect results, every time.

Polenta roast potatoes

100ml duck fat or vegetable oil

8 large baking potatoes, such as
Rooster, peeled

sea salt

8 tbsp polenta

The ability to make a great roast potato is key to being a great cook. I use polenta, a ground cornmeal, to make the crispiest roast potatoes imaginable. The recipe may seem short, but follow the steps and timings carefully to achieve perfection.

1 Preheat the oven to 200°C.
2 Place the duck fat or oil in a baking tray and put it in the oven.
3 Bring the potatoes to the boil in a pan of generously salted water, then simmer for 5 minutes.
4 Strain off the water, leaving the potatoes in the pan, cover with a cloth and leave to steam for 2 minutes so they go soft on the outside.
5 Add the polenta and a pinch of salt to the pan, put on the lid and shake the pan to bash the potatoes together until they become fluffy and coated in the polenta.
6 Add the potatoes to the hot oil and cook for 45–50 minutes, turning regularly, until they are crisp and golden brown.

Mashed potatoes

8 large baking potatoes, such as
    Rooster, with skins on
100g rock salt
300ml double cream
300g cold butter, diced
salt and freshly ground
    black pepper

This is the best of Ireland in a bowl: potato, cream, butter, salt. I make my mash using potatoes baked on salt. This draws out any excess water as they cook, resulting in the creamiest mash you've ever tasted. Don't be shy on the butter.

1 Preheat the oven to 200°C.
2 Place the potatoes on a bed of rock salt on an ovenproof tray. Prick with a knife before baking for 1 hour. The skin will be crispy and the pulp inside soft.
3 Place the cream in a small saucepan and heat until steaming.
4 Remove the potatoes from the oven, cut in half and press the pulp through a potato ricer, leaving the skins behind. If you don't have a ricer, scrape the flesh out of the skins and mash thoroughly with a potato masher. There can be no lumps here.
5 Place the dry potato pulp in a pan on the heat and gradually add the cream. Finally, add the butter, mixing all the time, until you have a shiny mash.
6 Season with salt and pepper and serve warm.

Perfectly cooked rice

200g basmati rice
200ml boiling water
I tbsp sea salt

You'd be surprised how many times rice isn't cooked properly when it seems so simple. You can use a rice cooker, but they take up a lot of space. Here's a fool-proof recipe using a steamer, a bowl and the kettle that will guarantee perfectly cooked rice every time.

I Start by heating a steamer pot with boiling water in the base. In a small heatproof bowl, add equal volumes of boiling water and rice. Whatever the quantity, the ratio is 1:1.
2 Place the heatproof bowl on the steamer insert and cover with a lid for 15 minutes until the water in the bowl has been absorbed and the rice is cooked through.
3 Remove carefully from the steamer and fluff with a fork. Serve warm.

Classic omelette

3 large eggs
2 tbsp single cream
1 knob of butter
sea salt

I started working in a Michelin-starred kitchen when I was 18. Every new commis chef had to cook a classic omelette for the chef on their first day. This was seen as the true test of skill and detail. Mine did not pass the test! 'I cannot serve this to a guest,' was the chef's reaction. In hindsight, nobody ever created an omelette good enough for his guests, so maybe that was all part of the show? Anyway, this recipe gives a pretty detailed guide to making a classic omelette, so hopefully yours will pass with flying colours.

1   You need a non-stick pan for this recipe. If you are not sure your pan is non-stick, cover the pan in table salt and place on a high heat for 10 minutes until the salt is smoking. Discard the salt, brush away any excess, and your pan will become non-stick for about 3 omelettes.
2   Put the eggs and cream in a jug or bowl and use a fork to whisk together until smooth. Season with salt.
3   Heat the pan over a medium heat, add the butter and allow it to melt but not brown.
4   Pour in the egg and cream mixture and begin shaking the pan, using a spatula to pull the cooked outer area into the centre of the pan.
5   After about 30 seconds, stop using the spatula and gently rotate the pan until the uncooked egg on top begins to set.
6   Lift the handle and let the mixture move to the far side of the pan. It should be slightly loose but softly set nearest to you.
7   Starting at the far edge, begin folding the egg mix over on itself, like rolling a carpet, until you reach the slightly wet centre, then fold the cooked egg over the top.
8   Turn the omelette upside-down onto a plate and serve warm.
9   The perfect omelette should be smooth, pale yellow in colour and shaped like a rugby ball.

6 large eggs

I thumb-sized slice of 'nduja
    sausage

2 slices of sourdough bread

butter, for spreading

I tbsp crème fraîche

I pinch of salt

Scrambled eggs on toast with 'nduja

The keys to perfect scrambled eggs are high-quality, fresh eggs; folding them while they cook; and taking them off the heat before they are ready, to finish in the residual heat of the pot. Here I've added some 'nduja for spice and colour and a touch of crème fraîche for a luxurious finish.

I   Put the eggs in a bowl and whisk with a fork until the whites and yolks have incorporated.

2   Heat a non-stick pan and add the 'nduja. Cook over a medium heat to release the spices and oils into the pan, breaking it up with a spatula.

3   Toast the sourdough slices in the toaster, then coat in a thin layer of butter.

4   Next, add the eggs to the pan. Continue to cook over a medium heat, folding the eggs over themselves using a spatula.

5   Once the eggs begin to set slightly, remove the pan from the heat and stir in the crème fraîche. Season with salt at this point; if you season too early, the eggs begin to separate.

6   Spoon the eggs onto the toast and serve warm.

Pan-roasted root vegetables

2 tbsp vegetable oil

4 carrots, cut into batons

4 parsnips, cut into batons

I tbsp plain flour

3 star anise

80ml sherry vinegar

80ml maple syrup

sea salt

One of the questions people regularly ask is how to make crispy roast vegetables. It's not in the nature of some vegetables to go crispy, so you're already struggling. A dusting of flour can help, and I like to treat them like meat and cook them all the way in the pan. You'd be surprised how quickly they cook once you control the temperature. A little sweet and sour vinegar and maple syrup at the end makes them sing.

I Heat a large, non-stick pan over a medium heat and add the oil.

2 Dust the prepared vegetables in the flour, which will stick to the damp exterior.

3 Put the carrots in the pan first and cook for a few minutes until they begin to colour all over.

4 Add the parsnips and the star anise and fry until both begin to soften and caramelise. Manage your heat at this point – the vegetables need to cook through without burning on the outside.

5 Add the vinegar and boil to reduce it to almost nothing, then add the maple syrup and continue to reduce until you have a thick glaze that coats the vegetables. Season with salt and serve.

Perfect white fish

100g salt

1 litre water

1 thick cod fillet, bones and skin
   removed

3 tbsp vegetable oil

How do you cook fish properly? How do you stop it from falling apart in the pan? Follow these simple steps. The bath in salt water will firm up the flesh and season the fish, while the rolling will tighten the flesh so it doesn't fall apart. Fish doesn't take long to cook, so only keep it for a few minutes in the pan.

1   Whisk the salt into the cold water until it has completely dissolved.
2   Take the fillet of cod and remove any of the thinner belly side of the fillet. Place the fish into the salt water and soak for 20 minutes.
3   Remove from the water and pat dry. Roll the fish lightly in clingfilm to create a sausage shape, then chill in the fridge overnight.
4   Next day, cut the fish into slices and remove the clingfilm; the slices should each be around 150g in weight.
5   Place a frying pan over a medium heat and add the oil. Place the fish flat-side down and cook for 3–4 minutes until golden brown before flipping it over to cook for 1 more minute.
6   Serve the fish immediately.

Perfect chicken breast

Serves 4

3 tbsp vegetable oil

4 chicken breasts, skin on

sea salt

This is one of the most common ingredients in our fridges, but how do you cook it perfectly every time? Crispy skin is a must.

1 Preheat the oven to 180°C.
2 Place an ovenproof non-stick pan onto the stove and add the oil. Place the chicken breasts onto the cold pan skin-side down and press with your hand to flatten the skin underneath. (Don't forget to wash your hands after.)
3 Now turn onto a medium heat and season with salt. Cook the chicken for about 5 minutes until the skin is evenly golden brown and the outside of the flesh is beginning to turn white. Don't turn the breasts.
4 Take the whole pan and place it in the oven for 5–7 minutes, depending on the thickness of the breasts. They should turn white all over and be firm to the touch.
5 Remove from the oven and flip the breasts to reveal the evenly golden brown, crispy skin. Add a touch more salt, slice and serve.

Part Two: Lighter Dishes

This chapter covers a bit of everything – from breakfast, brunch, and lunches perfect for those 'working from home' days, to summer salads and some more upmarket starter-style dishes. There are even a few light and fresh main courses. Basically, some inspiration for when you want maximum flavour without the threat of a food coma!

Salmon gravadlax with warm blini

For the salmon

I medium-sized salmon fillet,
  boned and cleaned, with skin on
300g sea salt
100g caster sugar
zest of I lemon
a little olive oil
I large bunch of dill, chopped
freshly ground black pepper

For the blini

250ml milk
2 tsp fast-action dried yeast
  (I sachet)
160g wholemeal flour
I tsp caster sugar
I tsp sea salt
3 egg whites
I egg yolk
200ml blonde lager
75g plain flour
butter, for cooking
sea salt
sour cream, to garnish

Curing your own salmon is easier than you might think, and you can ask your fishmonger to get the side of salmon ready to cure. The salt and sugar will work on the fish and is a form of cooking. The texture, colour and flavour will change and it will keep in the fridge for a few days after curing.

1   Place the salmon skin-side down on a large glass or ceramic tray. Don't use metal as it will react with the lemon.
2   Mix the salt and sugar in a bowl, add half the lemon zest and mix to a dry paste.
3   Rub this paste all over the salmon flesh, covering everything. Lay a tea towel on top and place in the fridge for 8 hours, or overnight, to allow the fish to cure.
4   The next day, run the salmon under cold water to wash off the excess salt, pat dry and place on a board.
5   Brush lightly with olive oil, then garnish with the dill, the remaining lemon zest and freshly ground black pepper. Run your knife along the base to remove the skin, then cut long slices of the flesh.
6   To make the blini, warm the milk to hand temperature before adding the fast-action yeast. Place the wholemeal flour, sugar and salt in a bowl and mix lightly before adding the milk mixture.
7   Bring the mix together using a spoon until a dough is formed, cover with clingfilm and leave at room temperature overnight.
8   The next day, whisk the egg whites until they form stiff peaks, then fold them gently into the dough before adding the egg yolk, lager, plain flour and salt; the mix will be quite liquid and airy.
9   To cook the blini, place a small non-stick pan on a low heat, melt some butter before filling the pan halfway with the mix. Cook over this low heat for about 10 minutes until the blini starts to rise and set. Flip and cook for a further 5 minutes.
10 Assemble the blini with some sour cream and pickled red onion, then top with sliced salmon.

Warm crab on toast

6 whole crab claws

2 slices sourdough bread

3 tbsp butter

½ garlic clove

a squeeze of lemon juice

sea salt

If you can get your hands on them, fresh crab claws are the nicest ingredient in the sea in my opinion. This is a dish to make an occasion of, take your time and try not to eat all the crabmeat before you get to plating the dish!

1 Bring a pan of water to the boil, season generously with salt and add the whole claws.

2 Depending on the claw size, cook in the boiling water for 6–10 minutes, then remove and leave to cool in a bowl for 30 minutes. As it cools it will continue to cook.

3 Using the back of a heavy knife, lightly crack the shells of the claws on the flat side to reveal the meat, then pull it off the cartilage, keeping it in large chunks.

4 Use a small metal skewer to push the sweet nuggets of meat from the knuckle shells. Once the meat is all removed, have a quick pick through it to catch any unwanted shards of shell.

5 At this point, toast the sourdough in the toaster.

6 Gently heat the butter in a pan and grate in the garlic. Once the butter is gently cooking the garlic, remove it from the heat and add the crab meat.

7 Place the sourdough on the plate and cover in the warm crab. Add a touch of lemon juice and salt to the leftover butter in the pan, swirl it round, then spoon this over the top so it soaks into the toast. Serve warm.

Classic prawn cocktail

300g raw peeled prawns
2 egg yolks
I tbsp Dijon mustard
I tbsp white wine vinegar
I tbsp Worcestershire sauce
I tbsp tabasco sauce
I tbsp brandy
300ml vegetable oil
3 tbsp tomato ketchup
I lemon, cut into wedges
½ head iceberg lettuce
I head baby gem lettuce
cayenne pepper, to taste
I handful of chives, snipped
sea salt and freshly ground
    black pepper

Another retro dish, and one that has stood the test of time for a reason. Quality prawns are a must, but a highly seasoned cocktail sauce packed with tabasco, Worcestershire sauce and brandy are what makes the prawn cocktail so memorable.

1 Place a small pan of water on the heat, season generously with salt and bring to the boil.
2 Drop the prawns in the water and cook for 1 minute only, until just cooked, then remove and chill in the fridge. The prawns need to be cold before they are dressed.
3 To make the sauce, put the egg yolks, mustard, vinegar, Worcestershire sauce, tabasco sauce and brandy in a blender and blitz to a paste. Then, with the motor still running, slowly pour in the oil until the sauce thickens.
4 Mix in the tomato ketchup and season to taste with salt and a squeeze of lemon juice.
5 Fold the sauce through the prawns, making sure they are just coated, not swimming in sauce. Set aside.
6 Slice the iceberg thinly, season with salt, pepper and lemon juice. Place in the base of the serving glasses.
7 Place some baby gem leaves around the edge of the glasses and fill the hollow with the dressed prawns.
8 Top with cayenne pepper and chives, and garnish with a wedge of lemon.

Crispy skinned salmon with tenderstem broccoli and green sauce

4 salmon steaks, cleaned and
  boned
a dash of vegetable oil
I tsp caster sugar
20 tenderstem broccoli stalks
I handful of parsley
I handful of mint
I handful of dill
2 tbsp capers
50g tin of anchovies, drained
I green chilli
5 tbsp olive oil
zest and juice of I lemon
sea salt

With salmon, it's important to try and source the best quality possible. There are many questionable versions out there. The technique here will result in crispy skin every time. Adding a small amount of sugar when blanching broccoli and other greens, like sprouts, will really bring out the flavour and prevent any bitterness.

1   Line a baking tray with baking parchment, then put the salmon steaks skin-side down on top, sprinkle them with salt and leave in the fridge for 1 hour.
2   Preheat the oven to 180°C and place a pan of water on the heat to boil.
3   Before cooking the salmon, cut 3 shallow lines lengthways along the skin. This stops the skin from curling and allows the flesh to cook more quickly.
4   Place a non-stick, ovenproof frying pan on a medium heat and add a little oil. Before the pan heats up, place the salmon in the pan skin-side down. Apply a small amount of pressure on the salmon for a minute as the skin begins to fry; this will keep it flat.
5   Leave the salmon on a medium heat for 3 minutes before transferring the pan to the oven. Don't flip the fish. Cook for a further 3–4 minutes in the oven. Remove the pan from the oven and then flip the fish to reveal the crispy skin. Leave to rest for 5 minutes before serving.
6   Meanwhile, season the boiling water with salt and sugar, and cook the broccoli for 3 minutes.
7   While the broccoli is cooking, add the herbs, capers, anchovies, chilli and olive oil to a blender and blend to a smooth paste. Season with the zest and juice of a lemon and some salt.
8   Remove the broccoli from the water and dress with the green sauce, top with the crispy skinned salmon and serve.

Seafood chowder

Serves 4

50g butter
500ml fish stock
I onion, diced
2 garlic cloves, sliced
3 celery sticks, diced
I large potato
I leek, finely sliced
80g plain flour
I large glass white wine
200ml single cream
200g white fish, skinned and
   boned
200g salmon, skinned and boned
I large handful of mussels, cleaned
   and bearded
200g prawn tails
I tbsp Dijon mustard
juice of I lemon
I large handful of dill
I large handful of chives
sea salt

Great chowder should be packed with seafood –
many aren't despite the name! If you don't have fish
stock you can use chicken, and the fish only needs
a few minutes to poach in the soup. This is a great
lunch option with some brown bread.

1 Place a large, heavy-based saucepan on a medium heat, add
   the butter and allow it to melt.
2 Heat the fish stock to just below boiling.
3 Add the vegetables all at once and cook gently over a medium
   heat for 3–4 minutes until everything begins to soften.
   Season with salt.
4 Increase the heat, add the flour and cook it out, stirring for
   1 minute before adding the white wine.
5 Add the fish stock and allow it to reduce by a third before
   adding the cream.
6 To prepare the fish, dice the white fish and salmon into
   thumb-sized chunks, check the mussels for any beard or
   shell.
7 Add the fish, mussels and prawns all at once. Simmer for
   5 minutes until the mussels open and the fish is fully cooked
   through. Discard any mussels that remain closed.
8 Finish the chowder by seasoning with Dijon mustard, salt
   and lemon juice. Chop the dill and chives and fold through
   at the last minute before serving.

Sausage and egg muffin

For the muffins

140ml milk

1 tsp fast-action dried yeast
   (½ sachet)

200g plain flour, plus extra for
   dusting

2 tsp caster sugar

½ tsp salt

25g butter, melted

oil, for greasing

For the sausage patty

100g pork mince

50g sausage meat (removed from
   your favourite brand of pork
   sausage)

1 tsp salt

1 tsp dried rosemary

1 tbsp vegetable oil

4 eggs

4 slices of Cheddar

This will probably look familiar but we're using some slightly higher-quality ingredients. While working at a highly acclaimed restaurant back in the day, Saturday morning treats included a large bag of these – they were an absolute joy with a strong black coffee.

1 Start with the muffins. Warm the milk to just above hand temperature and add the fast-action yeast, then leave it to sit for 1 minute.

2 Put the flour, sugar, salt and butter in a mixer bowl with the dough hook, then add the milk and yeast. Knead for 5 minutes until you have a soft, sticky dough. If you are working by hand, bring the dough together in a bowl before tipping out onto a lightly floured surface and kneading for about 10 mins.

3 Transfer to a greased bowl and leave in a warm place to double in size. This should take about 45 minutes.

4 Once doubled in size, turn out onto a floured work surface and roll out to about 3cm thick using a rolling pin.

5 Use a cutter to cut into circles the width of a mug and place them onto a tray dusted in flour. If you don't have a cutter you can use a mug and a small knife.

6 Cover the muffins with a cloth and leave to double in size again (another 45 minutes or so).

7 Heat a non-stick pan over a low heat, add the muffins to the dry pan, cover with a lid and cook for 4 minutes on each side. The steam created by the lid helps them rise. Remove and reserve for later.

8 To make the sausage patties, mix the pork mince, sausage meat, salt and dried rosemary. Shape into thin patties about 1cm thick. Heat a non-stick pan and add 1 tablespoon of vegetable oil, then add the patties and cook for 1 minute on each side until golden brown.

9 Once the patties are cooked, fry the eggs in the same pan for 2 minutes on both sides until the egg yolk has just set.

10 Slice the muffins in half and toast them, then assemble with the patties, cheese and egg. Serve immediately.

Ratatouille tart

Serves 4

For the tomato jam

I tbsp olive oil

4 garlic cloves, sliced

I large onion, diced

I tbsp tomato paste

100ml white wine vinegar

50g caster sugar

400g tin of chopped tomatoes

I courgette

I red pepper

I yellow pepper

I aubergine

2 medium tomatoes

I large disc of ready-made puff
    pastry, about 25cm in diameter

I egg yolk

50g halloumi, diced

For the glaze

5 tbsp olive oil

I tbsp Dijon mustard

I tbsp white wine vinegar

I handful of basil leaves,
    to garnish

Ratatouille is steeped in culinary folklore; it was also a fantastic film! Served as a tasty puff pastry tart, this is perfect for a light lunch or dinner party starter. The jam can also be made in a large batch and will keep in the fridge for weeks.

1   Preheat the oven to 200°C. Place a baking tray in at this point to warm it up.

2   Begin by making the tomato jam. Put the olive oil in a pan over a low–medium heat and cook the garlic for a few minutes until golden brown.

3   Add the onion and cook for a few minutes to colour, then follow with the tomato paste, vinegar and sugar. Simmer, stirring, until thickened and reduced by half.

4   Once reduced, add the chopped tomatoes and cook until it is a thick jam-like texture. Cool, then chill; this can keep in the fridge for weeks.

5   Slice the courgette, peppers, aubergine and tomatoes into even discs, about 2cm thick.

6   Place the pastry disc on a circular sheet of baking parchment. Brush the disc with an egg yolk and cover the base with the cooled tomato jam.

7   Using the jam circle as a guide, assemble the vegetable slices in a ring, continuing until they meet in the centre.

8   Carefully move the tart onto the preheated tray in the oven. Use the baking parchment under it to move it. Cook for 25 minutes until the pastry is golden brown and the vegetables are soft and golden brown.

9   Whisk the olive oil, mustard and vinegar in a bowl, then brush over the top of the tart.

10 Place the halloumi on a dry pan and chargrill on both sides. Add this to the top of the tart and garnish with basil leaves.

11 Serve in the centre of the table to share.

Shakshuka with chorizo and spiced hummus toast

2 tbsp vegetable oil

I garlic clove, sliced

½ onion, finely diced

50g chorizo

400g tin of chopped tomatoes

I00g roasted red peppers,
     drained and sliced

4 large eggs

For the hummus

400g tin of chickpeas

4 tbsp sesame oil

juice of I lime

I tbsp harissa paste

sea salt

4 slices of sourdough

This is a really quick dish to throw together for breakfast or brunch. For me, hunting the nuggets of chorizo is the best part. While I have added the recipe for a simple homemade hummus, you can always buy a quality one to make life easier.

1 Preheat the grill to high.
2 Heat a non-stick pan and add some vegetable oil over a medium heat. Add the garlic and onion and fry gently until softened but not browned.
3 Dice the chorizo into thumbnail-sized chunks and add to the pan. Cook this for 1 minute to release the oil before adding the tinned tomatoes.
4 Roughly slice the peppers and add them to the pan. Cook the mix gently over a low heat for 15 minutes, stirring occasionally, until you have a thick sauce consistency. Remove from the heat and create 4 holes using a spoon.
5 Crack the eggs into the holes and return to a medium heat to cook. Cook the eggs for 2 minutes on the heat so the egg white sets.
6 Once this happens, place the whole pan under the grill for 1 minute or so to cook the egg yolk lightly and bubble the sauce.
7 To make the hummus, simply put the chickpeas, sesame oil, lime juice, harissa paste and salt in a blender and blend to a paste. You can adjust the texture with more sesame oil if you wish, just be aware it might take more seasoning.
8 Toast the sourdough and smear with the hummus. Serve alongside the baked eggs.

Potato rosti
with poached egg

2 large floury potatoes, such as
    Rooster, peeled
I tbsp plain flour
I egg yolk
vegetable oil, for frying
4 fresh, medium-sized eggs
2 tbsp mayonnaise
tabasco sauce
sea salt

The key to rosti is in squeezing out all the flavourless liquid from the grated potato. The key to a perfect poached egg is super-fresh eggs where the yolk is encased in jellied white, and rapidly boiling water to create a teardrop shape.

1   Preheat the oven to 200°C.
2   Lay the potatoes on a tea towel or cloth on the work surface. Using a box grater, grate the potatoes onto the towel.
3   Wrap the potatoes in the towel and squeeze out any excess liquid before placing in a bowl.
4   Add the flour, egg yolk and salt to the bowl and mix it all together so it begins to stick.
5   Heat a non-stick pan and add a little oil. Roughly shape the rostis into flat circles about 2.5cm thick using your hands, then add them to the pan.
6   Cook over a medium heat for 3 minutes on each side until they are golden brown and soft throughout. If they are still raw inside, you can pop them in the hot oven for 5 minutes to cook through.
7   To poach the eggs, place a pan of water on the heat and bring to the boil. Add the eggs one by one, wait 30 seconds until the egg white sets, then reduce the heat slightly to a simmer. Cook for 2 minutes for a soft poached egg.
8   Place the rostis on the plates, add a dollop of mayonnaise, followed by the poached eggs. Season with salt and a few drops of tabasco and serve.

Serves 4

Fish fingers
with tartare sauce

For the cod

500g cod, skinned and boned

50g plain flour

2 eggs, mixed in a bowl with a
    splash of milk

100g dried breadcrumbs

100ml vegetable oil

sea salt

For the tartare sauce

1 egg yolk

1 tbsp Dijon mustard

1 tbsp white wine vinegar

300ml vegetable oil

4 tbsp chopped capers

4 tbsp chopped gherkins

1 handful of parsley

zest and juice of ½ lemon

This is the perfect way to introduce kids (or adults!) to eating fish. They'll look like the product from the packet but this is real food. I've used cod here, but any white fish will do; you can even ask your fishmonger to prep and portion the fish. I've made a classic tartare sauce from scratch, but nobody will care if you jazz up a pre-made mayonnaise. Summer on a plate.

1 Portion the cod into long strips about the size of your longest finger and lay them out on a baking tray.

2 Sprinkle a light dusting of sea salt on the fish and leave in the fridge for 30 minutes. Remove the fish and dry lightly on a cloth.

3 Lay out a breadcrumbing station: a plate of flour, a shallow bowl of milk and eggs whisked together, then a plate of breadcrumbs.

4 Coat the fish in the flour, followed by the egg wash and then the breadcrumbs. Repeat the process again to make sure the fish is completely covered. Set aside in the fridge.

5 To make the sauce, mix the egg yolk, mustard and vinegar in a bowl. Whisking the mixture continuously, slowly add the oil until it forms a thick mayonnaise.

6 Fold the capers, gherkins, parsley and lemon zest through the mayonnaise and season with salt and lemon juice.

7 To cook the fish fingers, pour the oil into a non-stick pan and place over a medium heat. Lay the fish fingers into the pan and cook for 2 minutes on each side until golden brown and cooked through. Remove and season with salt and pepper. Garnish with parsley and serve with the tartare sauce.

Herb-crusted cod with boiled new potatoes

800g cod, skinned and cleaned

I tsp sea salt

I handful of parsley, plus extra,
   chopped, to garnish

I handful of chives

100g Parmesan, grated

200g stale bread, chopped

zest of ½ lemon

10 new season potatoes, such as
   Queens

a knob of butter

sea salt and freshly ground
   black pepper

Herb-crusted fish is a mainstay of restaurants around the world and is a really simple and tasty way of showcasing fresh fish. By adding salt in advance, you draw out some of the moisture from the flesh, making it firm and flaky once cooked.

1   Place the cod on some baking parchment on a baking tray. Sprinkle with the salt, then leave in the fridge for 2 hours before patting the flesh dry with a paper towel.

2   Preheat the oven to 180°C.

3   In a food processor, blend the parsley, chives, Parmesan and bread until it is bright in colour, fine in texture and slightly soft to the touch. Season with salt, pepper and a little of the lemon zest.

4   Simmer the potatoes in heavily salted boiling water for 15 minutes until just soft. Strain and return the potatoes to the pot, glaze with some melted butter, herbs, sea salt and lemon zest.

5   Place the fish on fresh baking parchment on an ovenproof tray, then cover in the green breadcrumbs. Pat the crumb down so it completely covers the fish.

6   Cook for 20 minutes in the preheated oven, then leave to rest for a further 5 minutes.

7   Serve the fish alongside the potatoes.

Chicken satay skewers

1 thumb-sized piece of ginger root

3 garlic cloves

1 tbsp light soft brown sugar

1 tbsp light soy sauce

6 tbsp chunky peanut butter

1 medium red chilli

1 tbsp curry powder

1 tbsp ground cumin

4 chicken breasts, cut into chunks

a dash of vegetable oil

100ml coconut milk

1 tsp cornflour

1 lime

sea salt

1 handful of roasted peanuts,
   crushed

Peanut butter can be used on more than sandwiches – and here's the proof. These are great as a snack, as a starter or alongside some garnishes as a main meal. The leftovers also make a great roll filling with ripped coriander leaves and sriracha sauce.

1   Preheat the grill to the highest setting. Line a roasting tray with some kitchen foil to catch the marinade.

2   Remove the skin from the ginger and slice the outer layers off, leaving behind the fibrous centre. Put the ginger in a blender with the garlic, sugar, soy sauce, peanut butter and chilli.

3   In a dry pan, mix the curry powder and cumin and toast lightly until smoking, then add this to the blender and blend to a paste.

4   Place the chicken breast chunks in a bowl and add half the marinade from the blender, mix through, then leave to marinate for at least an hour, preferably overnight.

5   Thread the chicken chunks onto metal skewers, making sure to leave a small gap in between each piece so they cook evenly.

6   Place under the grill and cook for 2–3 minutes on all sides until they are charred and cooked through.

7   While the skewers grill, place a frying pan on a medium heat with a little oil. Add the remaining marinade and cook out for 2–3 minutes, stirring occasionally.

8   Mix the coconut milk and the cornflour and add this to the pan. Bring the sauce to the boil and adjust the seasoning with lime juice and salt.

9   Finish the skewers by brushing with the sauce and topping with some crushed roasted peanuts. Serve warm.

Chicken Kiev

4 chicken breasts (about
    200g each)
4 eggs
200ml milk
2 tbsp plain flour
200g dried breadcrumbs
100ml vegetable oil

For the butter
150g soft butter
4 garlic cloves, crushed
1 tbsp finely grated Parmesan
1 handful of parsley, chopped
sea salt and freshly ground
    black pepper

A little extra work, yes, but this recipe repays you with tonnes of flavour and value. I usually make the Kievs in advance and keep them in the fridge. The biggest fear with them is that they burst and fall apart when you're frying, but by breadcrumbing twice they hold together perfectly. Much better than anything you'd buy in a tray!

1   Preheat the oven to 180°C.
2   Start by making the butter: put the butter, garlic, Parmesan and parsley into a bowl and mix together. Season with a pinch of salt and set aside.
3   Remove the inner fillet from the chicken. Make an incision along the side of the breast. Don't go through the other side or to the ends of the breast. You should have a hollow pocket that's easy to fill.
4   Fill the pocket with the garlic butter, enough to just reach the edge of the pocket, then chill the breasts in the fridge.
5   Set up a breadcrumbing station: whisk the eggs and milk together to create a wash. Sprinkle the flour on a plate and season with salt and pepper. Put the breadcrumbs on another plate.
6   Toss the breasts in the seasoned flour, then coat in the egg wash, followed by the breadcrumbs. Repeat the process again to create a thick layer of breadcrumbs that seal in the open side of the chicken breast. Pinch the gap to make sure it's tight.
7   Shallow-fry the breasts in the oil in a non-stick pan for 2 minutes on each side over a medium heat. The oil should not be too hot so that the chicken cooks through and goes golden brown all over.
8   Remove the evenly golden breasts from the pan and place in an ovenproof tray. Cook for a further 8 minutes in the oven before serving piping hot.

Barbecued beef koftes with tzatziki and flatbreads

For the kofte
I tbsp ground cumin

I tbsp ground coriander

I tsp dried chilli flakes

3 cardamom pods, grated

600g beef mince

sea salt

For the flatbreads
300g strong plain bread flour,
   plus extra for dusting

I tsp fast-action dried yeast
   (½ sachet)

2 tbsp olive oil, plus extra for
   greasing

30g yogurt

I pinch of sea salt

150ml warm water

For the tzatziki
I cucumber

250g yogurt

juice of ½ lemon

2 tbsp olive oil

I tsp chilli flakes

I handful of mint leaves, torn,
   plus extra to garnish

I handful of dill fronds, torn,
   plus extra to garnish

This is a different way of using up your trusty beef mince. Cardamom pods are a spice I always keep in the store cupboard and are magic here. The flatbread is a great vessel for catching all the juice from the kofte and tzatziki, and it is one I use for a variety of dishes.

1. To make the flatbreads, put the flour, fast-action yeast, olive oil, yogurt and salt into a mixer, bind together slowly. Now, with the motor running, add the warm water in a steady stream until it starts to come together into a wet dough.
2. Knead the dough for 5 minutes at a medium speed until it cleans the bowl. If you are doing this by hand it might take a little longer.
3. Place in a greased bowl, cover and leave in a warm place for 1 hour to double in size.
4. Once the flatbread dough has doubled in size, knock it back on a floured surface. Using a rolling pin, roll until it is 1cm thick, cut into even-sized breads and cook for 1 minute on each side in a smoking hot non-stick pan. They should blister and bubble as they cook. Set aside.
5. To make the tzatziki, peel the cucumber and cut into dice about the size of your small fingernail. Season the yogurt with lemon juice and salt and cover the cucumber dice. Drizzle with olive oil and sprinkle with chilli flakes before topping with the roughly torn mint and dill.
6. To make the kofte, using a dry pan, toast the spices for 1 minute until smoking, then tip them into a bowl with the beef mince and salt and mix until well blended. Mould the spiced meat around 4 metal skewers. They should be even in thickness around the skewer.
7. Cook on a hot barbecue or in a griddle pan for 2 minutes on each of the 4 sides until cooked through and charred all over.
8. Assemble the flatbreads with koftes, tzatziki and some more herbs.

Part Three:
Quicker Dishes

These are my midweek meals, designed to be thrown together with ingredients from the fridge after a day at work. Expect plenty of store cupboard ingredients for bursts of flavour. A few of these recipes can also be batch-cooked and double up as lunch the next day, which is always a lifesaver. You'll also find some fancier dishes that are sure to impress at the weekend, but won't see you stuck in the kitchen all day.

Soufflé pancakes with crispy bacon and maple syrup

300g self-raising flour
2 tsp baking powder
100g caster sugar
4 eggs, separated
360ml milk
1 tbsp vegetable oil
8 slices streaky bacon
3 tbsp maple syrup

Bear with me on this one. It may seem a little fiddly to separate the eggs and whisk the whites, but it's worth it. It also brings a little chef magic to a simple dish. If I'm honest, I'm not a big fan of pancakes but adding American-style bacon and maple syrup will usually turn my head.

1 To make the pancake batter, mix the flour, baking powder and 50g of sugar in a bowl.
2 Next, add the egg yolks and milk and mix to a rough paste.
3 In a separate bowl, whisk the egg whites until they form soft peaks when the whisk is lifted out of the mixture. Continue to whisk as you gradually add the remaining 50g of sugar until stiff peaks are formed and the mixture sticks to the whisk.
4 Gently fold the egg whites into the batter by turning the mix over on itself, keeping as much air as possible.
5 Heat a non-stick pan on a low heat and add a splash of oil.
6 Place a large ladle of the mixture in the far side of the pan, then work clockwise round the pan to add 2–3 more pancakes, depending on the size of your pan. Cover with a lid and cook for 3–4 minutes.
7 Turn the pancakes in the order you put them in the pan, then cook for 1 more minute. The mixture will gradually rise.
8 Remove the pancakes from the pan and keep them warm in a very low oven or on a heatproof plate set over a pan of hot water while you cook the remainder.
9 While the pancakes are cooking, fry the bacon in a non-stick pan until crispy.
10 Stack the pancakes, top with bacon and drizzle with maple syrup to serve.

Quick pan pizza

Makes 4 individual pizzas

For the dough

300g strong plain bread flour,
plus extra for dusting

3 tsp fast-action dried yeast
(1 ½ sachets)

1 tsp sea salt

2 tbsp olive oil, plus extra
for greasing

2 tbsp yogurt

150ml hand-hot water

For the quick tomato sauce

8 large tomatoes, halved

1 pinch of sea salt flakes

1 tsp dried mixed herbs (such as
oregano, rosemary, thyme)

3 garlic cloves, whole with
skins on

2 tbsp olive oil

1 tbsp tomato paste

sea salt

For the toppings

50g mozzarella

50g chorizo

rocket leaves, to garnish

salt and freshly ground
black pepper

Few of us have a pizza oven in our back garden, so using a pan is a great way of getting something similar with day-to-day equipment. The key is the crispy base and quick cooking time. This is a great weekend activity where everyone can make their own. You can keep the rolled dough balls in the fridge for 24 hours, if you want, and the tomato sauce freezes really well.

1 To make the dough, use your hands to mix the flour, fast-action yeast and salt together in a bowl. If using a mixer, bring together using a dough hook attachment.

2 Now mix the olive oil, yogurt and warm water together, pour into the bowl and bring the mixture together into a wet dough. Tip the dough onto a clean work surface lightly dusted with a little flour and knead by hand for 3 minutes until the dough forms a smooth ball (or the mixer will do this for you).

3 Put the dough in an oiled bowl and cover with a cloth. Leave in a warm place for 1 hour to double in size.

4 Preheat the oven to 200°C.

5 To make the simple tomato sauce, season the tomatoes with the salt and dried herbs, place on a baking tray with the garlic cloves and drizzle with the olive oil. Roast for 30 minutes.

6 Squeeze the pulp from the garlic into a blender or flat-based bowl, discarding the skins, then spoon in the tomatoes and tomato paste. Blend or use a potato masher to blend to a rough sauce consistency. Any extra will hold well in the freezer.

7 Now back to the dough. Tip it out of the bowl onto a floured work surface and knock it back lightly with your hands. This means pushing it to take out some of the air; it should return to a flatter square about 7.5cm thick.

8 Cut the dough into quarters and roll into 4 roughly shaped balls. Cover again and leave it to rise for another 30 minutes.

9 Now it's pizza time! Flatten the dough balls into discs about 1cm thick, wide enough to fit neatly into the non-stick pan you are going to use. >

10 Before assembling, preheat the grill to the highest setting. Get a non-stick pan or shallow cast iron pot onto the hob on a high heat. Once the pan is smoking, dust it with some flour, add your dough and leave it to sit for 30 seconds.

11 Spread the dough with tomato sauce and finish with whatever toppings you like. I like mozzarella and chorizo. Try not to overload the dough so you can achieve a crispy base. Then fire the pan under the grill for 2 minutes, or until golden and bubbling.

12 Remove from the grill, top with fresh rocket and slice.

Spaghetti with crispy bacon, garlic and chilli

200g dried spaghetti

4 tbsp olive oil

100g rindless streaky bacon,
   cut into lardons

3 garlic cloves, crushed

2 chillis, finely diced

50g Parmesan, grated

juice and zest of 1 lemon

1 large handful of freshly
   chopped parsley

salt and freshly ground
   black pepper

This is a dish I usually throw together late at night or after work. It uses the usual suspects from a sparse fridge and cupboard – pasta, bacon (or rashers if you're local!), garlic cloves, chilli and Parmesan – and can be made in 15 minutes if you move. Chilli flakes can be used instead of fresh chilli, and the key point is not to overcook your spaghetti.

1 Place the pasta in a pan of boiling, salted water and cook until just tender. This takes about 8 minutes.
2 As the pasta is cooking, get a wide-based, non-stick pan on a medium heat and add the oil.
3 Add the bacon and fry until just crispy and golden. Reduce the heat slightly and add the garlic and chillis. Cook for about a minute until the garlic starts to turn golden.
4 Next remove the pasta from the water and add to the pan with a ladleful of the starchy pasta water. Season with the Parmesan, lemon juice, zest and chopped parsley.
5 To finish it off, increase the heat again and cook for 1 minute, keeping the pasta moving, until a glossy, starchy sauce is formed.
6 Adjust the seasoning with salt and pepper and serve in warm bowls.

Spaghetti carbonara

160g spaghetti

3 egg yolks

30g Parmesan, grated, plus extra
   to serve

50g thick-cut bacon, cut into
   lardons

freshly ground black pepper,
   lemon and salt, to season

Classic Italian carbonara consists of pasta, egg yolk, black pepper, guanciale (cured pig jowl), pecorino cheese and water. The cream-like sauce consistency is achieved through the gentle heating of the egg yolk and pasta water in the pan. I've swapped guanciale and pecorino for bacon and Parmesan as they are a little more accessible. This is one of the great dishes of the world.

1   Place a pan of boiling, salted water on the heat. Add the spaghetti and cook for 8 minutes until just tender.
2   Crack the egg yolks into a bowl, then season with pepper, Parmesan, lemon juice and salt.
3   Place a non-stick frying pan on a medium heat and cook the bacon for about 5 minutes until crispy. Reduce the heat to low.
4   Remove a ladleful of the pasta water and mix it into the egg yolks. Add the spaghetti to the pan containing the bacon lardons and all the fat. Make sure the heat is really low.
5   Now add the egg yolk and water mix and begin tossing and moving the pasta in the pan for 1 minute until a glossy, thick sauce is formed and coating the pasta.
6   Finish with some more grated Parmesan and pepper, then serve warm.

Prawn and clam linguini with garlic, chilli and parsley

200g spaghetti

5 tbsp olive oil, plus extra to finish

3 garlic cloves, crushed

1 chilli, finely diced

100g clams

12 prawns, peeled and cleaned

20g Parmesan, grated

zest and juice of 1 lemon

1 large handful of parsley, chopped

sea salt

A *vongole* in Italian, but my version includes prawns. I absolutely love prawns but feel free to leave them out. This is a quick dish to prepare that feels a little more sophisticated. Sit back and pretend the sun is shining on your back somewhere on the Amalfi coast.

1 Place the pasta in boiling, salted water and cook until just tender. This takes about 8 minutes.

2 Meanwhile, in a non-stick frying pan, heat the olive oil over a medium heat. Add the garlic and chilli and cook for 2 minutes or until the garlic has started to turn golden.

3 Add the clams and prawns and season with salt.

4 Remove the pasta from the water and add to the pan with the seafood. Add a ladleful of pasta water, followed by the Parmesan, lemon zest and juice, and the parsley. Cook over a high heat until the sauce thickens and glazes the spaghetti. This takes about 2 minutes.

5 Season with some more olive oil, lemon and salt and serve in warm bowls with a spoon to get the last of the sauce.

Mushroom and Parmesan spaghetti

50g wedge Parmesan, broken into
  chunks, plus extra to serve

5 tbsp dried mushrooms

250g spaghetti

100g wild mushroom selection
  (oyster, shitake, chestnut),
  finely sliced

lemon juice, to season

sea salt and freshly ground
  black pepper

I love this dish – it's so simple to make but so delicious. Dried mushrooms are available in most supermarkets and make a fantastic sauce or stock. It still puts a smile on my face when the blender turns the watery, cheesy broth into a silky, shiny sauce worthy of any restaurant kitchen. Folded through pasta with some extra seasoning, this is a winner.

1 Put the Parmesan chunks in a saucepan, add 700ml of water and bring to the boil. Reduce the heat to a simmer and add the dried mushrooms. Turn off the heat and leave to infuse for 30 minutes until the Parmesan breaks down and the liquid turns brown in colour. It will look odd at this point but stick with it!

2 Cook the spaghetti in boiling, salted water for 8 minutes until just tender.

3 Heat a non-stick frying pan over a medium heat and fry the wild mushrooms for about 5 minutes until golden brown and wilted.

4 The Parmesan and mushroom stock will have reduced to about 500ml. Discard the outer hard layer of the cheese and place all the ingredients in a blender. Add a ladle of the pasta cooking water and blend to a smooth and creamy sauce. Adjust the seasoning with salt, lemon juice and black pepper.

5 Fold the sauce through the cooked and drained spaghetti, and top with more Parmesan and the fried mushrooms.

Spaghetti Bolognese

Serves 6

2 tbsp vegetable oil

800g beef mince

1 onion, finely diced

4 garlic cloves, minced

2 carrots, finely diced

3 celery sticks, finely diced

80g bacon lardons

2 tsp chilli flakes

1 handful of thyme leaves

1 handful of rosemary leaves

2 tbsp tomato paste

50g Parmesan, including the rind,
    plus extra to serve

400ml red wine

2 × 400g tins of chopped
    tomatoes

1 beef stockpot

1 tbsp Dijon mustard

500g spaghetti

1 handful of parsley, chopped

sea salt and freshly ground
    black pepper

This is how I make Bolognese sauce. The key here is taking the time to properly brown your mince. The more colour you get, the better the flavour will be at the end. The addition of the Parmesan rind adds some flavour that would otherwise end up in the bin. This recipe is large to allow for leftovers. I make quick meals in the days after by adding it to baked potatoes or spreading it in a roll with rocket and Parmesan.

1   Heat a heavy-based, flameproof casserole dish over a high heat. Add 2 tablespoons of oil and leave it to get hot. Add the mince and break it up, allowing it to brown heavily all over. This will take about 5 minutes. You will need to do the mince in 2 batches to maintain the heat in the pan. Once it is all browned, leave the mince aside on a plate until later.

2   In the same pan, add the onion, garlic, carrots, celery and bacon with another tablespoon of oil and begin to colour all over.

3   Add the chilli flakes, thyme, rosemary, tomato paste and Parmesan rind and cook for a further 2 minutes to soften it all down. It should be just starting to stick to the base of the pan.

4   Increase the heat, add the wine and boil to reduce to almost nothing as you scrape the crispy bits from the base of the pan with a wooden spoon.

5   Next, return the browned mince to the pan before adding the chopped tomatoes, stockpot and mustard. Reduce to a simmer, place a lid on the pan and cook for 30 minutes until it's all melted together into a delicious sauce.

6   Meanwhile, cook the spaghetti in boiling, salted water for 8 minutes until just tender, then drain.

7   Season the sauce with salt and pepper and finish with the parsley. Don't forget to remove the Parmesan rind before serving, folding some of the sauce through the spaghetti. Plate everything up and finish with more grated Parmesan and serve warm. Pack the leftovers in lunch boxes for the fridge.

Paella

Serves 2

3 tbsp olive oil, plus extra to serve

4 garlic cloves, sliced

I tbsp 'nduja sausage

3 tbsp smoked paprika

I tin anchovies

150g paella rice

200ml white wine

600ml chicken stock

I pinch of saffron strands

100g monkfish, cut into chunks

200g prawns, shelled

200g mussels, cleaned and
  bearded

100g squid, cleaned and sliced

I lemon, cut into wedges

I handful of parsley

crusty bread, to serve

I'd like to introduce this recipe by stating this is not your traditional paella. I made the mistake of cooking this on Spanish TV, then ended up with an avalanche of strongly worded emails. Worse, I had to copy and paste the emails in Google Translate, making the process even more painful. Anyway, what I will say is it's absolutely delicious, great for impressing at the weekend, and you only have one pot to clean at the end! *P.S. If you did email to complain, I haven't had time to respond!*

1   Put the olive oil and garlic in a heavy-based pan and cook over a medium heat for a few minutes until the garlic starts to brown.

2   Add the 'nduja, stirring while it melts down and cooks out for 1 minute.

3   Add the smoked paprika and anchovies and cook for 1 minute.

4   Add the rice and stir to coat in the flavoured oil. Keep it over a medium heat for 1 minute, then add the wine. Keep stirring gently for a few minutes. Once the wine has disappeared, it's time to add the stock and saffron.

5   Cook over a medium heat until the stock reduces and the rice appears from the liquid. Shake the pot every minute. It should take about 10 minutes for the rice to cook and the stock to almost evaporate.

6   Add the seafood and submerge it in the liquid and rice, place the lid on and shake the pot. Cook for a further 3 minutes until the mussels are opened and the prawns turn pink. Discard any mussels that remain closed.

7   Finish with some lemon wedges, parsley, more olive oil, smoked paprika and sea salt to taste. Serve to share from the same pan with some crusty bread.

Perfect simple risotto

2 tbsp vegetable oil

2 shallots, finely diced

I garlic clove, diced

160g Arborio rice

300ml dry white wine

I litre warm chicken stock

50g Parmesan

I tbsp freshly ground black pepper

20g butter, diced

sea salt

There's a common misconception that risotto takes hours to make, while slaving over a pot, stirring. Yes, you must stir, but the rice will only take 12–15 minutes to cook over a high heat, allowing the stock to reduce and intensify in flavour as it cooks. This is a simple risotto using cheese and pepper but the method is the same for a variety of flavours. Focus on the timings and you'll be amazed by the results.

1 Heat a heavy-based saucepan over a medium–low heat, add the vegetable oil, and softly cook the shallots and garlic without adding any colour.

2 Once softened, sprinkle with salt, add the rice and cook over a medium heat for 1 minute.

3 Increase the heat before adding the white wine, then simmer until it disappears.

4 Add the stock a ladleful at a time over a high heat, waiting for it to be absorbed before adding more, until the rice is just softened but hasn't turned to mush. It should only take 12 minutes from wine to finish. It's important to have the heat high so the flavour concentrates while the rice cooks.

5 Add the last ladle of stock so the mix is soup-like in texture. Finish by adding the grated cheese, pepper and butter.

6 Mix this through and allow the risotto to rest for 2 minutes so it thickens. Adjust the seasoning with salt and lemon juice and serve warm.

Thai green chicken curry

500g skinless and boneless
    chicken thighs

2 tbsp sea salt

100ml vegetable oil

I green pepper, diced

2 onions, roughly chopped

100g green beans

2 tbsp white wine vinegar

300ml coconut milk

300ml chicken stock

50g spinach leaves

I handful of coriander leaves

For the spice paste

2 tbsp ground coriander

2 tbsp ground ginger

2 tbsp ground cumin

3 green chillis

8 dried lime leaves

I lemongrass stick

I thumb-sized piece of ginger root

I onion

4 garlic cloves

2 green peppers, seeds removed

zest and juice of 2 limes

2 tbsp vegetable oil

5 tbsp fish sauce

2 tbsp honey

Perfectly cooked rice (page 15), to
    serve

While you can, of course, buy a quality green curry paste, it's very easy to make one at home using a blender (I even leave the skins on, you won't notice!). I use chicken thighs here as they are more cost effective and have better flavour than breast. This is a recipe packed with taste that won't take hours to make.

1   Lay out the chicken thighs on a cloth, season all over with the salt and leave to sit for 30 minutes.

2   To make the paste, toast the coriander, ground ginger, cumin and chilli in a non-stick hot pan for 1 minute until it starts to smoke, then tip into a blender.

3   Add the lime leaves, lemongrass, ginger root, onion, garlic, green peppers, lime juice and zest, vegetable oil, fish sauce and honey to the blender. You do not need to remove the skins. Blend to a smooth paste. This can be used straight away or frozen in small bags for later use.

4   To cook the curry, heat a large, heavy-based saucepan over a high heat, add the oil and let it get smoking hot. Add the green pepper and onions and fry for a couple of minutes to colour, then add the green beans.

5   Stir in the curry paste and cook out over a high heat for 2 minutes, keeping everything moving so it doesn't burn.

6   Next, add the white wine vinegar and stir for a minute until it evaporates.

7   Now add the coconut milk and stock, bring to the boil, then turn the heat right down until the curry is simmering.

8   Slice the chicken thinly, add it to the pan and poach gently for 10 minutes.

9   Finish with the spinach and fresh coriander and adjust your seasoning with honey, lime, salt and fish sauce to taste. Serve with steamed rice.

Chicken nuggets with roasted garlic mayonnaise

50g plain flour

3 tbsp egg wash (I egg and
  IOOml milk)

50g breadcrumbs

I tbsp ground cumin

2 tbsp vegetable oil

4 chicken breasts, diced into
  large chunks

For the garlic mayonnaise

I head of garlic

a dash of olive oil

I egg yolk

I tbsp Dijon mustard

I tbsp white wine vinegar

300ml vegetable oil

a dash of lemon juice

a sprinkling of cayenne pepper

a few snipped chives

sea salt

A dish we will all have seen before – but done properly. A touch of cumin in the breadcrumbs is a winner. The roasted garlic for the mayo is a handy trick for lots of dishes.

1   Preheat the oven to 150°C.
2   To start the garlic mayonnaise, sit the head of garlic on a piece of kitchen foil, add some salt and olive oil and wrap into a parcel. Bake for 50 minutes until the garlic is soft inside.
3   Set up a breadcrumbing station: lay out a shallow bowl with flour, one with egg wash and one with breadcrumbs seasoned with cumin.
4   Roll the chicken chunks in the flour, followed by the egg, followed by the breadcrumbs. Repeat this process a second time, then set the nuggets aside in the fridge until you are ready to cook.
5   To make the mayonnaise, remove the garlic head from the kitchen foil, slice the bottom and squeeze the softened pulp into a bowl. Turn up the oven temperature to 180°C.
6   Add the egg yolk, mustard and vinegar to the garlic and whisk into a paste. Slowly add the vegetable oil, whisking continuously, until you have a thick mayonnaise. Adjust the seasoning with salt and lemon juice.
7   Garnish the mayonnaise with some cayenne pepper and chopped chives and use as a dip for the nuggets.
8   To cook the nuggets, heat a frying pan with some vegetable oil and cook the nuggets for about 8 minutes until golden brown on all sides. Transfer to a baking tray and bake for 5 minutes, depending on the thickness, until cooked through. Serve warm.

Chicken, broccoli and bacon crumble

500ml chicken stock

50g butter

50g plain flour

400g tin of condensed chicken
   soup

1 tbsp Dijon mustard

1 tbsp curry powder

juice of 1 lemon

1 handful of tarragon leaves,
   chopped

500g leftover mixed bread:
   sliced pan, sourdough, brioche,
   brown bread

2 tbsp vegetable oil

100g butter

100g Parmesan, grated

400g chicken breast, diced

200g bacon lardons

400g broccoli, diced

sea salt and freshly ground
   black pepper

baked potato and salad, to serve

Another single from my mother's greatest hits, this dish was regularly rolled out at important family events. It remains a hit in our house today, usually served with a baked potato swimming in butter. Be mindful not to use a dish that's too deep or else it won't cook evenly in the centre.

1   Preheat the oven to 200°C and warm the chicken stock.
2   Melt the butter with the flour in a large saucepan over a high heat and cook for 1 minute until the mix is bubbling, stirring continuously. Pour in all the chicken stock and whisk constantly until the mix comes to the boil and thickens.
3   Remove from the heat, add the condensed soup, mustard, curry powder, lemon juice and tarragon, then season to taste with salt and pepper.
4   Using a food processor, blend the leftover bread until it forms chunky breadcrumbs.
5   Heat a non-stick pan, then add the oil. Add the breadcrumbs and butter, season with salt and pepper and cook for a few minutes, stirring, until light golden brown. Drain off any excess oil, then grate in the Parmesan.
6   To assemble, put the diced chicken breast, bacon lardons and broccoli into a shallow casserole dish; the depth is important so that it cooks evenly.
7   Spoon over the sauce, and then top with the fried breadcrumbs.
8   Cook at 200°C for 1 hour. If the topping begins to colour too much, cover with kitchen foil for the rest of the cooking time. Leave to rest for 15 minutes before serving. Perfect with a baked potato and simple salad.

Roast chicken and quick gravy

1 brown onion, quartered with
  skin on

1 head of garlic, halved

1 large free-range chicken
  (typically 1.5–2kg)

a dash of olive oil

1 small glass of white wine

600ml chicken stock

1 tbsp soft butter

2 tbsp plain flour

3 sprigs of fresh thyme

1 tsp Dijon mustard

sea salt and freshly ground
  black pepper

Day one in cooking college involved a roast chicken. Crispy skin, moist meat and soft legs are essential. The chicken will create its own sauce base as it roasts – we just help it on its way at the end with some thickening and seasoning.

1 Preheat the oven to 200°C.

2 Spread the onion quarters and garlic halves on a heavy-duty roasting tray.

3 Pat the chicken skin dry, then place on the onion and garlic mix, brush with some olive oil and then season liberally with sea salt and black pepper.

4 Roast the chicken for 1 hour, then leave to rest in the tray for 10 minutes.

5 At this point, we can make the quick gravy. Remove the chicken carefully from the tray and place on a chopping board. Place the roasting tray on the heat. If you don't want to cook in the tray you can pour the contents into a pan.

6 Increase the heat and add the white wine, get a wooden spoon into the tray and scrape all the colour and juices from the bottom.

7 Now add the chicken stock and bring to the boil. Mix the soft butter and flour together to create a paste. Add this to the boiling mix and whisk constantly until it begins to thicken.

8 To finish, pass the gravy through a sieve to remove the vegetables, making sure to squeeze all the juice from the mix. Season with some fresh thyme leaves, mustard and some salt and serve alongside your roast chicken.

Barbecue chicken tikka skewers

4 large chicken breasts

I tsp chilli powder

I tsp paprika

I tbsp garam masala powder

I tsp ground coriander

I whole red chilli

I thumb-sized piece of ginger root

5 garlic cloves

6 tbsp thick natural yogurt

sea salt

zest and juice of I lime

I handful of coriander leaves, ripped

Have a large batch marinating in the fridge so you can pull them out midweek and cook them for a quick lunch or dinner. The yogurt acts on the breast meat as it marinates, adding flavour and tenderising the meat. If you don't have time to barbecue, they'll work just as well cooked in a hot non-stick pan.

1 Dice the chicken breasts into thick, thumb-sized chunks before placing in a bowl.

2 Place a small pan on a medium heat and add the chilli powder, paprika, garam masala and ground coriander. Toast for 30 seconds to liven it up before tipping into a blender.

3 Add the whole chilli, ginger and garlic cloves along with the yogurt and blend to form a smooth paste.

4 Mix into the chicken chunks and leave to marinate for at least an hour but ideally overnight.

5 Thread the chicken onto metal skewers, leaving a small space between each piece so the chicken cooks evenly.

6 Preheat a barbecue on full flame for 15 minutes so the grates become non-stick. Cook the skewers for 3–4 minutes on all sides until the outside of the chicken is blackened and charred and the meat cooked through.

7 Remove from the heat and season with salt, lime juice and zest, and some ripped coriander leaves.

Yuk sung with peanut slaw

400g pork mince

4 tbsp vegetable oil

3 garlic cloves, grated

1 thumb-sized piece of ginger
   root, peeled and grated

1 tbsp dried chilli flakes, plus
   extra to garnish

1 ½ tbsp dark soy sauce

2 tbsp oyster sauce

3 spring onions, sliced

zest of ½ lime

8 iceberg lettuce cups

For the slaw

1 carrot

1 green apple

4 white cabbage leaves

1 tbsp peanut butter

1 tbsp Dijon mustard

2 tbsp white wine vinegar

100ml olive oil

4 tbsp roasted peanuts

sea salt and freshly ground
   black pepper

Yuk Sung is a great midweek recipe for keeping people happy and fed, without slaving for too long. The pan, store cupboard and grater will do the heavy lifting for you. Depending on how hungry the crowd are, you can serve with lettuce cups and/or rice.

1   Heat a non-stick pan over a high heat, add the pork mince and break it up using a wooden spoon so that it browns all over. It's very important to let the mince sit and caramelise, so don't keep moving it.

2   Make a well in the middle of your pan and add the vegetable oil, garlic, ginger and chilli flakes. Cook for a few minutes until the garlic turns golden, then stir it into the mince.

3   Reduce the heat slightly, then add the soy sauce and oyster sauce. Mix to coat the pork and cook for a further minute until it becomes sticky.

4   Turn off the heat completely and garnish with the spring onions, some more chilli flakes and the lime zest.

5   To make the slaw, begin by grating the carrot and apple into a bowl, using a box grater, or else slice thinly with a knife.

6   Next, slice the cabbage as thinly as possible and add this into the bowl.

7   For the dressing, whisk together the peanut butter, mustard, vinegar and olive oil. Season with salt and pepper. Pour this into the slaw mix and dress. Top with the toasted peanuts before serving up with the mince and the lettuce cups.

Quick beef chilli with pico de gallo salsa

2 tbsp vegetable oil

500g lean beef mince

1 beef stock cube

1 onion, diced

2 garlic cloves, diced

1 red pepper, diced

10 jalapeños, diced

1 red chilli, diced

1 tbsp chilli flakes (or less if you
  don't like the heat)

1 tbsp ground coriander

4 tbsp soy sauce

400g tin of black beans, drained
  and rinsed

2 eggs

freshly ground black pepper

For the salsa

5 tomatoes, quartered and
  deseeded

½ onion, diced

1 tsp ground cumin

1 tsp chilli flakes

zest and juice of ½ lime

a small handful of chopped
  coriander leaves

sliced avocado, to serve

Perfectly cooked rice (page 15),
  to serve

I'm not sure when or why I started adding eggs to this dish, but it bulks it up using a cheaper ingredient and really blends all the big flavours together. Either way, it's very tasty, particularly when you use grated stock cube as a seasoning! I'll often make a bit extra and reheat it with nachos and melted cheese for the weekend.

1   Begin by heating a large non-stick pan. Cook the mince in the oil over a medium–high heat until well coloured all over; it will take about 5 minutes.

2   Season the mince by grating in the beef stock cube and adding some red pepper.

3   Now for the vegetables, get the onion, garlic, red pepper, jalapeños, chilli and spices into the pan and allow to colour over a high heat for a few minutes, stirring well.

4   Season with the soy sauce, then add the beans and reduce the heat to low.

5   Crack the eggs into the pan and mix through the mince. This will make sure the spicy flavours really blend with the mince.

6   To make the salsa, chop the deseeded tomatoes into small dice before adding the diced onion. Season the salsa with the cumin, chilli and zest of lime. Finish with the juice and some chopped coriander.

7   Serve in warm bowls with some steamed rice.

Steak au poivre

2 tbsp vegetable oil

2 x 300g well-aged fillet steaks

100ml Cognac

2 tbsp freshly ground
    black pepper

2 tbsp red wine vinegar

400ml single cream

2 large knobs of butter

1 tbsp pickled green peppercorns
    (if you can't get these, just add
    another tbsp of black pepper)

lemon juice, to season

sea salt

One of the all-time great dishes. If you don't have green peppercorns, you can just add another tablespoon of black pepper. It's a brilliant date-night dish, if you're that way inclined, or one for the weekend. If you don't want to use fillet steaks, look at ribeye or flank steak instead. By the way… if you're in Paris, Bistrot Paul Bert make the best version of this dish I've ever eaten.

1   Heat a non-stick pan until it is smoking hot, then add the oil. Season the steaks liberally with sea salt, then brown on all sides in the pan.

2   Now reduce the heat slightly and keep turning the steaks every 30 seconds. Managing the heat is key. Use a cake tester or metal skewer to check the internal temperature of the steak. When medium rare, the skewer should be slightly warm to touch on your lip. Remove the steaks and leave to rest for 5 minutes on a plate.

3   While the steak is resting, pour the Cognac into the pan. Be careful if you are using a gas hob as the Cognac will briefly ignite. Next, add the black pepper and vinegar and cook it out for a minute until it has almost evaporated. Add the cream and cook it out until it has reduced by half before adding the butter and green peppercorns. Cook over a high heat for 2 minutes, or until a thick sauce-like consistency is achieved.

4   Now, return the steak to the pan with all the resting juices from the plate. Coat the steaks in the sauce, season with a touch of lemon juice and serve warm.

Mick's Finnish meatballs

2 onions, finely diced

2 tbsp vegetable oil

400g beef mince

400g pork mince

2 egg yolks

1 tsp white pepper

2 tsp allspice powder

1 tbsp sea salt

5 tbsp breadcrumbs, soaked in
   100ml milk

2 knobs of butter

5 tbsp malt vinegar

500ml single cream

juice of ½ lemon

1 handful of dill fronds, torn

sea salt and freshly ground
   black pepper

For the cucumber pickle

1 cucumber

2 tbsp malt vinegar

1 tbsp caster sugar

Mick is a world-renowned chef. He hails originally from Finland but, having spent more than half his life in Ireland, his accent lands somewhere between Helsinki and Headford. These meatballs were a staff meal hall of famer, creamy and savoury with malt vinegar and dill.

1 Add the onion and 1 tablespoon of oil to a large pan and sweat over a low–medium heat for 2 minutes until they just begin to soften but don't begin to colour. Tip into a bowl and set aside to cool slightly.

2 Add the beef and pork mince, egg yolks, white pepper, allspice and salt to the bowl. Squeeze any excess milk from the breadcrumbs and add this before mixing thoroughly.

3 At this point, wash your hands. Now keep them wet while you roll the meatballs. This will stop the meat from sticking to your hands. The meatballs should be golf ball in size.

4 To prepare the cucumbers, slice them as thinly as possible and place on a tray. Season with the vinegar, sugar and salt and allow to marinate at room temperature for 30 minutes.

5 Place a heavy-based, non-stick pan on the heat, add the remaining oil and the butter and brown the meatballs on all sides for 2–3 minutes before transferring onto a plate.

6 Into the same pan, add the vinegar and cream and heat until simmering, scraping the caramelised meaty bits from the bottom of the pan using a wooden spoon. Return the meatballs into the sauce and cook over a high heat for 4–5 minutes, or until a thick, sauce-like consistency is achieved. The meatballs will cook through as the sauce reduces, thickens and glazes them. Turn them every minute as they cook.

7 Check the meatballs are cooked through by piercing with a metal skewer for 3 seconds. If the skewer is then hot to the touch, they are ready. You can add a little more cream and keep reducing if needed.

8 Remove the pan from the heat and finish with some lemon juice, the cucumber pickle slices, black pepper and ripped dill.

Rigatoni beef ragu

200g stewing steak, diced

200g beef mince

100g bacon lardons or pancetta

2 onions, finely diced

4 garlic cloves, crushed

2 tbsp dried chilli flakes (or less if you don't like the heat)

300ml red wine

3 tbsp water

1 heaped tsp cornflour

2 rich beef stockpots

2 tbsp soy sauce

250g tomato pasta sauce

250g tin of chopped tomatoes

400g rigatoni pasta

Parmesan, to grate

chopped parsley

I'm hoping this becomes the go-to recipe of this book as it's one I go to when I need a hug in a bowl. The magic moment involves cooking the pasta in the ragu sauce, allowing it to soak up all the goodness. And only one pot to clean up afterwards!

1   Preheat the oven to 180°C.

2   In a large, heavy-based, flameproof casserole dish, brown off the diced beef, minced beef and bacon or pancetta over a high heat until it's nice and golden brown. This will take a few minutes.

3   Add the onions, garlic and chilli flakes and cook for a further minute until they start to break down and soften. Keep the heat high to add some colour.

4   Add the wine and boil to reduce it by half.

5   Blend the water and cornflour to a paste, then stir it into the meat with the stockpots, soy sauce, tomato sauce and tomatoes and bring to the boil.

6   Place a lid on the dish and cook in the oven for 1 hour until the stewing steak is tender to touch.

7   Remove the dish from the oven carefully as it will be very hot. Add the dried pasta, and place back in the oven for a further 20 minutes until the pasta is soft and has soaked up all the sauce.

8   Serve the ragu in the pot, and finish with grated Parmesan and parsley.

Chinese stir-fried beef with soft boiled egg

2 tbsp vegetable oil

400g beef mince

2 tbsp dried chilli flakes

3 garlic cloves, crushed

I onion, sliced

I handful of green beans, halved

I green pepper, diced

½ head pointed York cabbage, finely sliced

6 tbsp oyster sauce

2 eggs

I tbsp sesame seeds, toasted

sea salt

Perfectly cooked rice (page 15), to serve

Oyster sauce is a good store cupboard ingredient to pick up and it brings all the flavours together nicely here. The trick with including the soft-boiled egg is one I use regularly to bulk up dinners or lunches. A good handful of dried chilli flakes at the end can fire this up nicely.

1 Heat a large non-stick pan over a high heat and add the oil.
2 Add the beef mince to the pan and caramelise heavily all over, breaking it up but trying not to move it around too much so it doesn't lose heat. Once brown, season with salt, then add the chilli flakes and garlic.
3 Now add the onion, green beans, pepper and cabbage. Cook for 2–3 minutes until they begin to soften.
4 Add the oyster sauce and mix through to glaze the mixture, adding a splash of water if you like it looser.
5 Add the eggs to a pan of cold water, bring to the boil, then cook for 5 minutes. Remove and run under the cold tap for 1 minute to release the shell, then peel. The shell should come away very easily but the egg should still be warm throughout.
6 Serve the beef mix in bowls, slice the egg and place half on top, then finish with toasted sesame seeds and chilli flakes. Serve with steamed rice.

Beef Stroganoff

Serves 2

1 tbsp vegetable oil

2 fillet steaks, cut into thick cubes

100g plain flour

1 knob of butter

12 button mushrooms, finely sliced

1 brown onion, finely sliced

3 garlic cloves

500ml beef stock

150g crème fraîche

1 tbsp smoked paprika

1 tbsp Dijon mustard

lemon juice

1 handful of parsley, chopped

sea salt and freshly ground
    black pepper

Perfectly cooked rice (page 15),
    to serve

This is a really old-school dish, the origins of which trace back to the chefs serving the Stroganov family in 19th-century Russia. A great recipe to throw together midweek, you can push the boat out and use fillet beef, but thick-cut striploin will work as well. Lots of seasoning is key, with the steamed rice lurking to soak up all that delicious sauce.

1 Place a non-stick pan on the heat and add the oil.
2 Dust the steak cubes with flour and season generously with salt and pepper.
3 Add the cubes to the pan with a knob of butter and cook over a high heat for 2–3 minutes, getting as much colour as possible. Remove the steak and leave it to rest on a plate. Drain any excess oil from the pan.
4 Add the mushrooms to the pan and cook them over a high heat for 2 minutes until they begin to colour, then add the onions.
5 As the onions cook, slice the garlic thinly, add this to the pan and mix.
6 Now add the beef stock and scrape the caramelised bits from the bottom of the pan using a wooden spoon. Continue to cook until reduced by half.
7 Next, add the crème fraîche and reduce by half again until the sauce starts to thicken.
8 Return the steak and resting juices to the sauce and simmer for 1 minute. Finish by seasoning with more black pepper, smoked paprika, mustard, lemon juice and parsley.
9 Serve classically alongside steamed rice.

Part Four: Longer Dishes

These are weekend dishes, when you have a little more time to commit to the kitchen. Don't get me wrong, they are still simple to cook and packed with flavour, but they require some time-consuming cooking techniques. Expect some braising, simmering, layering, glazing, slow-baking and, in the case of Beef Wellington, a two-day building project (absolutely worth it – just look at the photo!). This is your one-stop-shop for creating *haute cuisine* in the comfort of your own home.

My 'take' on bouillabaisse with rouille sauce

2 tbsp olive oil

1 fennel bulb, diced

1 onion, diced

4 garlic cloves, sliced

1 tbsp tomato paste

1 tbsp paprika

1 sprig of tarragon

200ml white wine

1 litre chicken or fish stock

400g tin of chopped tomatoes

1 tsp saffron strands

zest of 1 orange, plus a dash of
   juice

4 floury potatoes, such as
   Rooster, peeled and quartered

1 handful of mussels or clams,
   cleaned and bearded

1 handful of prawns, cleaned and
   peeled

1 handful of white fish, skinned
   and boned

juice of ½ lemon

For the rouille

50g cooked potato (from stew)

1 garlic clove, crushed

1 tsp saffron strands

1 tbsp white wine vinegar

1 egg yolk

200ml olive oil, plus extra for
   the baguette

salt and freshly ground
   black pepper

For the croûtons

1 baguette

Here's another French classic that's made for sharing. I'm calling it my 'take' on bouillabaisse so as to avoid grinding all the fish bones and flesh in the traditional recipe, which comes from the city of Marseille. This is a beautiful one-pot wonder and the rouille sauce thickens the stew as you eat it, pumping it with more flavour. Feel free to mix and match the fish as you please.

1   Preheat the oven to 180°C.

2   Place a large, heavy-based pan over a medium heat, add the olive oil and fennel and cook slowly without colouring for 1–2 minutes, then add the onion and garlic and cook for a few minutes until beginning to soften.

3   Increase the heat and add the tomato paste, paprika and tarragon.

4   Next add the white wine and reduce to a glaze. Add the stock and chopped tomatoes and bring to the boil.

5   Once boiled, reduce the heat to a simmer and add the saffron and orange zest. Add the potatoes and simmer for 25 minutes until the potatoes are just soft.

6   To make the croûtons, slice the baguette into thin slices and drizzle with olive oil, cook in the oven for 15 minutes until golden brown all over.

7   To make the rouille sauce, scoop out some cooked potato from the stew and place in a bowl, crush with a fork, season with crushed garlic, saffron and white wine vinegar and add the egg yolk. Whisking continuously, gradually pour in the olive oil until you have a thick sauce. Adjust the seasoning with salt and pepper.

8   Now back to the stew. Drop in the mussels, prawns and white fish. Simmer for 5 minutes until the fish is just cooked and the mussels have opened. Discard any that remain closed.

9   Adjust the seasoning with a touch of orange juice and lemon juice, and serve the stew in bowls, topped with the croûtons and rouille.

Pot-roasted cauliflower with spiced quinoa

2 tbsp vegetable oil

I large head of cauliflower

70g butter

I onion, finely diced

2 garlic cloves, sliced

3 tbsp ras el hanout spice mix

200g quinoa

300ml white wine

800ml vegetable stock

100g yogurt

20g sunflower seeds, toasted

I large handful of mint leaves

zest of I lime

sea salt

A vegetable-focused one-pot wonder. By roasting the cauliflower head whole, you can add layers of flavour and colour. It also looks pretty decent in the middle of the table, and can be served as a main dish, or alongside meat or fish.

1   Preheat the oven to 200°C.
2   Heat a large casserole dish over a high heat and add some vegetable oil.
3   Peel back the green leaves from the cauliflower and remove the thick base. Place in the dish and begin to get some colour on the exterior.
4   Once it begins to brown, drop the heat ever so slightly, add the butter and baste the cauliflower for 1 minute as it melts. Add the onion, garlic and spices, being careful not to let them burn, they need to be warmed and foaming, not smoking and frying.
5   After another minute, reduce the heat and add the quinoa into the base of the dish. Stir to coat it in the spiced butter, then add the wine and simmer to reduce it by half. Next add the stock and season with salt.
6   Put a lid on the dish and place in the oven for 30 minutes, or until the quinoa has absorbed the moisture, the liquid has disappeared and the cauliflower is soft.
7   Garnish with the yogurt, sunflower seeds, mint and lime zest.
8   Serve in the middle of the table to share as a whole meal, or even as a garnish.

Fish pie

There are hundreds of recipes for fish pie, so I've tried to keep this straightforward. In my opinion, the best fish pies are the ones that are jam packed with fish, not a pool of sauce under a sea of potato.

200g cod, skinned and boned
200g salmon, skinned and boned
200g smoked haddock, skinned and boned
200g prawns, shelled
100g frozen peas

For the sauce
1 onion, finely sliced
2 garlic cloves, crushed
300ml white wine
1 chicken stockpot
2 tbsp butter
3 tbsp plain flour
600ml milk
2 tsp Dijon mustard
zest and juice of 1 lemon

For the mash topping
10 large floury potatoes, such as Rooster
100ml warm milk
2 egg yolks
sea salt

1 Preheat the oven to 200°C. You'll need it preheated at this temperature for both the potatoes and the pie.
2 Start with the mash. Place the potatoes on an ovenproof baking tray, sprinkle a touch of sea salt on top of each one and bake for 50 minutes until the skin is crispy but the potatoes soft throughout.
3 Slice the potatoes in half. Spoon out the pulp and push through a ricer, otherwise use a masher by hand.
4 Place the dry mash in a saucepan over a low heat and mix in the warm milk, season with salt and finish with the egg yolks. Reserve for the top of the pie.
5 To prepare the fish, lay some paper towels on a plate and put the pieces of cod, salmon and haddock on top. Season with some sea salt and leave to sit in the fridge for at least 30 minutes.
6 Remove any excess salt and portion the fish into thumb-sized chunks. Lay them in a shallow, ovenproof baking dish. Cut the smoked fish into chunks and add it with the prawns. Pour in the frozen peas.
7 To make the sauce, put the onion, garlic and white wine in a saucepan over a low heat and simmer to reduce to a thickish glaze. Stir to mix in the stockpot.
8 In a separate pan, melt the butter over a low heat, then allow it to brown. Then increase the heat to high, add the flour and cook, stirring, for 1 minute.
9 Warm the milk gently in a microwave or on the hob, then gradually add it to the flour and butter in two stages, stirring with a whisk until smooth. Bring to the boil, then remove from the heat.
10 Season the sauce with your wine mixture, then finish with mustard, lemon zest and juice. Pour the sauce over the pie mix and fold it through with a spoon.
11 Spoon the mash on top and spike it up with a fork.
12 Bake for 1 hour until the top is golden brown and the mixture piping hot throughout.

Bacon and cabbage with parsley sauce

2kg unsmoked, boneless bacon
    joint
1 head of pointed or savoy
    cabbage
2 tbsp vegetable oil

For the sauce
500ml milk
1 tsp sea salt
100ml cider vinegar
60g butter
60g plain flour
2 tbsp Dijon mustard
½ chicken stockpot
1 handful of capers, chopped
50g parsley, chopped
a squeeze of lemon juice
sea salt and freshly ground
    black pepper

It's hard to beat bacon and cabbage. This recipe takes a little longer than some ways of cooking but results in beautifully textured bacon. You can pop it in the oven before you go to work, then come back to the deliciously moist bacon. Adding mustard and capers to the sauce packs the added punch that parsley can't offer you.

1   Take the bacon out of the fridge 30 minutes before cooking to bring it back to room temperature.
2   Preheat the oven to 200°C.
3   Wrap the bacon in 2 layers of kitchen foil so it's encased, then place on a baking tray. Bake for 5 minutes, then reduce the oven temperature to 80°C and cook for 6 hours.
4   Fast forward to about half an hour before the bacon is ready! Chop your cabbage into quarters. Heat a large non-stick frying pan over a high heat, add the vegetable oil and begin caramelising the cabbage on the flat sides. This should take about 5 minutes.
5   Remove the pan from the heat, place a lid on top and leave the cabbage to sit for 10 minutes. The residual heat and steam will cook the cabbage perfectly in this time. Before serving, season with salt.
6   Meanwhile, make the sauce. Warm the milk to just above hand hot and season generously with salt. Do not boil. Put the vinegar in a separate small saucepan and boil to reduce until it is almost gone. Add the butter and melt, followed by the flour. Cook this paste out over a high heat for 1 minute until it turns blonde in colour, whisking continuously.
7   Still whisking, gradually add the milk until it is all used and you have a thick sauce. Remove this from the heat and finish with the mustard, chicken stockpot, capers, parsley and lemon juice. Adjust the seasoning with salt and pepper and serve warm.
8   To serve up, slice the bacon and place on a sharing platter, dress with the cabbage quarters and finish with the parsley sauce.

Pad Thai

Serves 2

For the pan

a little vegetable oil

12 raw tiger prawns, deshelled

4 spring onions, roughly chopped

1 onion, finely sliced

2 eggs

1 handful of beansprouts

200g rice noodles, precooked

For the dried seasoning

1 tbsp vegetable oil, plus extra
    if needed

50g salted peanuts

4 garlic cloves, finely sliced

3 tbsp dried shrimps

1 tbsp chilli flakes

For the sauce

3 tbsp tamarind paste

3 tbsp light soft brown sugar

3 tbsp fish sauce

3 tbsp rice wine vinegar

3 tbsp water

For the garnish

1 red chilli, finely sliced

1 handful of mint leaves

1 handful of basil leaves

zest and juice of 1 lime

I've kept this recipe as authentic as possible. Some of the ingredients will have to be sourced in an Asian market but once you have them, you can make this again and again. This is Bangkok street food, so expect speed, big flavours, a touch of chaos and spice, and that feeling of wanting more … much like the city itself.

1   Begin by making the dried seasoning. Put the oil in a pan and begin roasting the peanuts for 1 minute, then add the garlic, dried shrimp and chilli flakes and cook until the nuts and garlic are golden brown. Add the mix to a blender with some extra oil, if needed, to loosen up, and blitz to a rough crumb texture. Set aside (this will also keep in the fridge for a few days).

2   Next prepare your sauce. Add the tamarind paste, sugar, fish sauce, vinegar and water to a pan and bring to the boil, then set aside for later.

3   Place a large non-stick pan on a high heat and have all your ingredients ready; this will all come together quickly! Add some oil and cook the prawns on both sides for 1 minute until pink. Next add the spring onions, onion, eggs and beansprouts along with half the dried seasoning and cook for 2 minutes until the egg is cooked and the vegetables golden. Fold in the precooked rice noodles and toss.

4   Now add the tamarind sauce and allow it to coat the noodles. Spoon the noodles into bowls.

5   Garnish the pad Thai with red chilli, mint and basil leaves, lime zest and juice along with the rest of the dried seasoning mix.

Butter chicken

400g skinless and boneless
   chicken thighs

100g natural yogurt

1 large thumb-sized piece of
   ginger root

1 whole red chilli

3 garlic cloves

1 tbsp garam masala

1 tbsp ground cumin

2 tbsp ground coriander

a dash of vegetable oil

For the sauce

70g butter, diced

1 onion, chopped

4 cardamom pods

5 garlic cloves, finely chopped

1 large thumb-sized piece of
   ginger root, finely grated

1 green chilli, finely chopped

1 tbsp garam masala

1 tsp ground cumin

2 tsp ground coriander

1 tsp chilli powder

4 tbsp tomato paste

250ml chicken stock

250ml double cream

lime juice

sea salt

Perfectly cooked rice (page 15),
   to serve

A staple of the Indian take-away menu, this dish comes under many guises. What makes this for me is the charred marinated exterior of the chicken swimming in the rich butter sauce. Use your blender to good effect here – it'll take on the heavy lifting.

1 Begin by cutting the chicken thighs into even but thick chunks.

2 Put the yogurt, ginger, red chilli, garlic, garam masala, cumin and coriander in a blender and blend to a paste. Pour this onto the chicken and leave to marinate for at least an hour, preferably overnight.

3 Heat a large flameproof casserole dish over a high heat and add the oil. Add the chicken pieces and cook for 2–3 minutes until they are charred on the outside. Carefully remove them from the dish and rest on a plate.

4 Now reduce the heat to medium and make the sauce.

5 Add a little of the butter to the dish followed by the onion, cardamom, garlic, ginger and chilli. Sweat this off for a minute.

6 Now add the rest of your spices: garam masala, cumin, coriander, chilli powder and the tomato paste. Cook this out for another minute.

7 Add the chicken stock and cream and bring to the boil. Return the chicken to the pan and simmer to thicken and reduce the sauce. Finally stir in the remaining butter to make it very luxurious.

8 Adjust the seasoning with lime juice and salt before serving with steamed rice.

Chicken and mushroom lasagne

4 large portobello mushrooms

I head of garlic

a drizzle of olive oil

I bunch of large-leaf spinach
    or cavolo nero

750ml milk

90g butter

I00g plain flour

I50g Parmesan or Gruyère,
    grated, plus extra to finish

400g tin of condensed chicken
    soup

2 tbsp Dijon mustard

zest and juice of ½ lemon

800g chicken breast, finely sliced

I pack of dried lasagne sheets

sea salt and freshly ground
    black pepper

Simple ingredients, big on flavour, and some handy shortcuts we won't tell anyone about. My mother always had a way of making magic with condensed chicken soup, so I've tried to do her cooking some justice here. It gives the sauce some serious flavour while maintaining the right consistency.

1   Preheat the oven to 150°C.
2   Place the portobello mushrooms, garlic head and some olive oil in a piece of kitchen foil and wrap tightly. Cook in the oven for 1 hour until the garlic pulp has gone soft in its skin.
3   Remove from the oven and slice the mushrooms and reserve the garlic head for the sauce later on. Increase the oven temperature to 190°C.
4   Next, remove the thick stalks from the spinach or cavolo nero, rip the leaves up into smaller pieces and set aside.
5   Warm the milk in a saucepan and season generously. Transfer to a bowl, then place the butter and flour into the same pan and cook over a high heat for 1 minute, whisking continuously, to cook out the flour.
6   Next, pour in the warm milk, still whisking continuously. It will begin to form a sauce immediately. Whisk the sauce up to the boil so it becomes glossy and shiny, with no lumps. Remove the pan from the heat and whisk in the grated cheese, condensed soup, mustard and lemon zest and juice.
7   Squeeze the garlic pulp into the sauce by removing the base of the bulb with a small knife and pressing the outer skin. Whisk this through thoroughly.
8   Layer the mix in an ovenproof lasagne dish: pasta sheets, sliced chicken, mushrooms, sauce, spinach or cavolo nero, repeat. Finish with a final layer of pasta, topped with sauce and more grated cheese.
9   Bake for 45 minutes, leave to rest for 15 minutes, then serve warm.

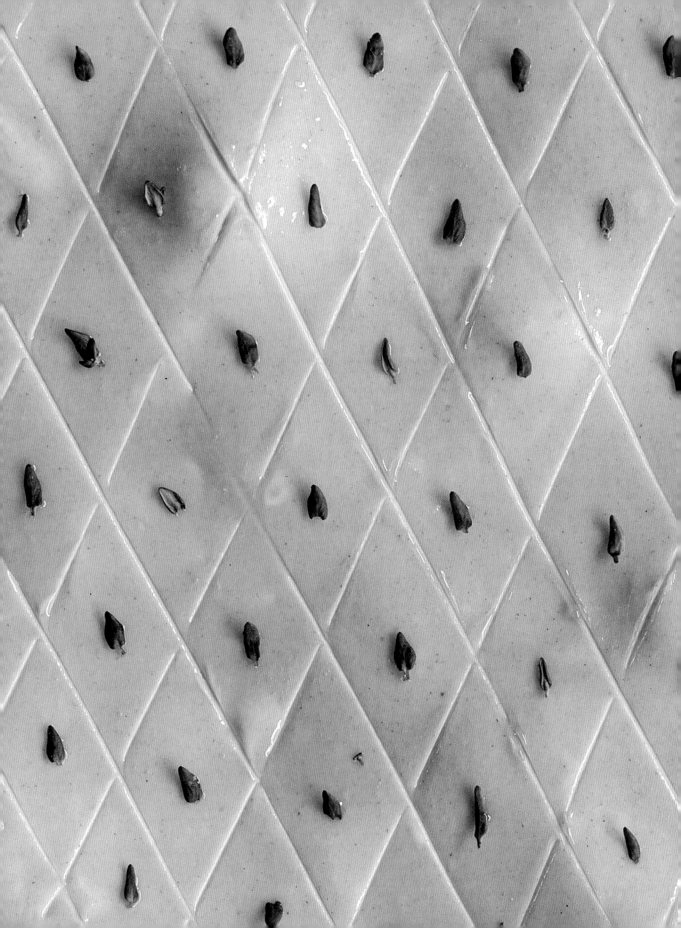

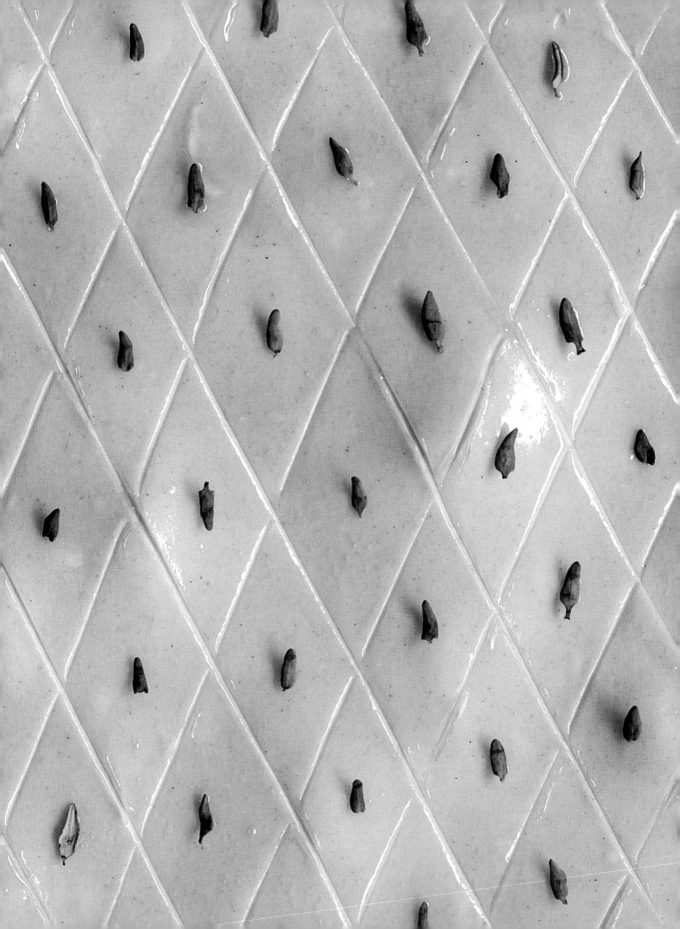

Chicken and leek pie

6 chicken breasts, diced into
   thick chunks

I onion, roughly diced

3 leeks, cleaned and sliced
   about Icm thick

100g butter

3 garlic cloves, thinly sliced

5 tbsp plain flour

I litre chicken stock

150ml single cream

I handful of tarragon leaves

I handful of thyme leaves

I tbsp wholegrain mustard

zest and juice of I lemon

I sheet ready-made puff pastry

I egg yolk

sea salt and freshly ground
   black pepper

Ready-made puff pastry can usually be found somewhere in my freezer. Here it's put to good use to create a pub classic. And who doesn't love when that golden-brown, savoury, crispy pastry dives deep into a creamy sauce to soak it all up?

1. Preheat the oven to 190°C.
2. Heat a heavy-based pan over a high heat and fry the chicken chunks for about 3 minutes to caramelise on all sides. Remove from the pan to rest on a plate. Warm up the chicken stock.
3. Add the onions and leek to the pan and begin to sweat over a medium heat, add a pinch of salt.
4. Next, add the butter and sliced garlic before adding the flour. Cook the flour for 1 minute over a high heat, stirring well.
5. Stir in the warm chicken stock and allow the mix to come to the boil and thicken into a paste. Stir in the cream and remove from the heat.
6. Return the chicken to the mix with the tarragon and thyme leaves, mustard, lemon zest and juice, and season with salt and pepper.
7. Transfer the finished mix to a baking tray and allow to cool slightly.
8. Roll out the puff pastry sheet and gently place this across the top of the mix. Pinch the edges so the pastry is secured to the tray. Brush with an egg yolk before adding a criss-cross design using a small, sharp knife.
9. Bake in the oven for 30 minutes until the pastry is dark golden brown and crispy, with the chicken cooked through.

Spicy Nashville fried chicken sandwich

Serves 4

For the chicken flour

200g plain flour

2 tsp sea salt

I tsp freshly ground black pepper

I tsp garlic powder

I tsp ground coriander

I tsp sweet paprika

For the burger

4 skinless and boneless chicken
   thighs

100ml vegetable oil

4 brioche buns

8 slices of white Cheddar

¼ iceberg lettuce, shredded

salt and freshly ground
   black pepper

For the burger sauce

2 tbsp mayonnaise

I tbsp tomato ketchup

I tbsp Dijon mustard

4 tbsp diced jalapeños

4 tbsp diced pickles

For the spicy seasoning

30g butter

I tbsp smoked paprika

I tbsp cayenne pepper

I tbsp garlic powder

I pinch of sea salt

In this recipe I try to replicate the famous sandwich from Belles Hot Chicken in Melbourne, Australia. I spent a year working in restaurants in Melbourne in 2017, and Sunday evenings consisted of sleeping, ordering these fried chicken sandwiches and watching *Law & Order* on TV … glamorous, I know! This recipe isn't perfect, but it's close!

1   Mix together all the ingredients for the chicken flour. Toss the chicken thighs in the flour mixture and shake off and reserve any excess, then set the chicken aside in the fridge for an hour to create a glue-like coating.

2   Remove from the fridge and re-coat the thighs in the flour.

3   Heat the oil in a non-stick pan until it sizzles when you add a sprinkle of the flour. Carefully add the chicken thighs and cook gently for 5 minutes on each side until cooked through, golden brown and crisp. To check the temperature, insert a metal skewer into the thickest part, then remove; it should be hot to touch.

4   Meanwhile, to make the burger sauce, mix the mayonnaise, ketchup, mustard, jalapeños and pickles. Halve the brioche buns and spoon some sauce onto the base of each bun.

5   To make the spicy seasoning, melt the butter, add the spices and cook over a medium heat for 1 minute. Remove the chicken from the pan when ready and turn it in the spiced butter to coat.

6   Place a hot chicken thigh on each bun base and top with two slices of cheese. Season the lettuce with salt and pepper and place it on the melting cheese. Top with the second half of the bun and serve.

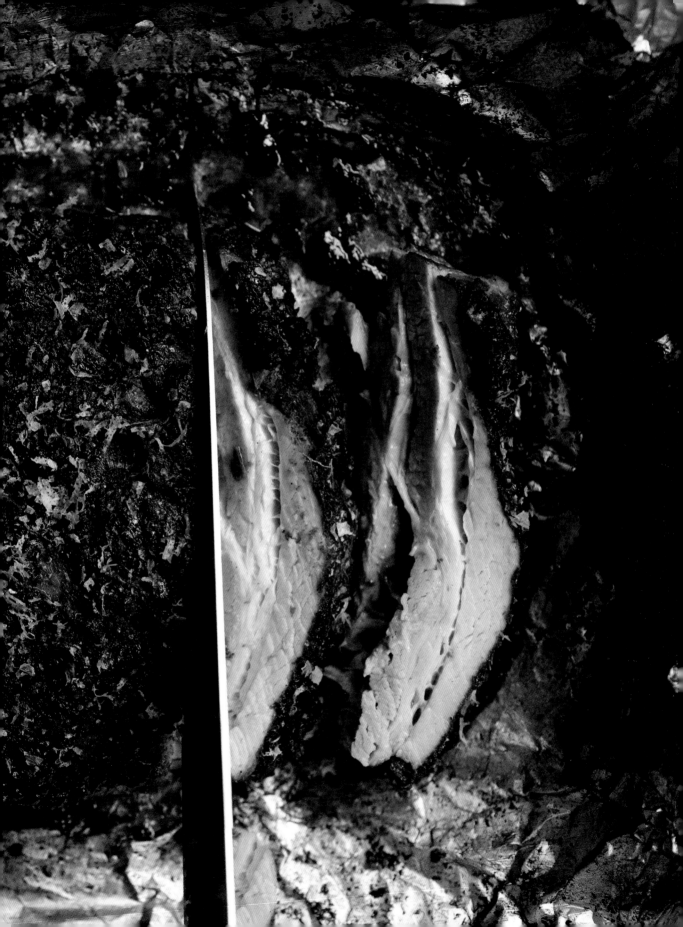

Spicy pork belly tacos with guacamole

1.5kg pork belly

zest and juice of 1 lime

For the marinade

3 onions, halved, with skin left on

5 garlic cloves

5 red chillies

2 star anise

3 tbsp cumin seeds

3 tbsp coriander seeds

1 thumb-sized piece of ginger root, grated

1 tbsp sea salt

3 tbsp white wine vinegar

For the salsa

½ red onion, finely diced

½ green chilli, finely diced

sea salt

For the guacamole

2 ripe avocados

1 tbsp tabasco sauce

1 handful of coriander

1 large tomato, deseeded and diced

sea salt and freshly ground black pepper

12 corn tortillas, to serve

A showstopper that's perfect for sharing but is still cost effective. I absolutely love landing this onto the table. Cutting the pork belly into thick chunks adds a sense of occasion to these tacos, packed with the good stuff: salt, fat, acid, heat.

1 Preheat the oven to 200°C.
2 Start by making the marinade. Place the onions, garlic, chilli, star anise, cumin and coriander seeds on an ovenproof tray and cook for 30 minutes until everything is softened and the skins nicely blackened.
3 Reduce the oven temperature to 150°C.
4 Place the roasted ingredients in a blender and season with ginger, sea salt and vinegar. Blend to a rough paste, adding a bit of water to loosen the mix if you need to.
5 Chill the paste slightly before smearing it over the pork belly and wrapping it all in kitchen foil. Make sure there are no gaps.
6 Place the foil package on an ovenproof tray and bake for 2½ hours until the meat is soft. Remove the foil and increase the oven temperature to 220°C for a further 10 minutes until the paste is charred across the top of the belly. Sprinkle with half the lime zest and some salt, then leave to rest for 15 minutes. Reserve the lime juice and remaining zest.
7 To make a quick salsa, mix the onion and chilli, then season with salt and a little of the lime juice, reserving the rest for the guacamole.
8 To make the guacamole, remove the skin and stone from the avocados. Mash the flesh with a fork, season with the reserved lime zest and remaining lime juice, the tabasco and salt. Mix and season to taste with salt and pepper. Fold in the tomato.
9 Back to the belly, cut it into good, thick chunks and serve to share, with warmed corn tortillas, and build to eat in your hands.

Porchetta

1 large pork belly, approx. 2kg in
    weight with bones removed

3 tbsp Dijon mustard

50g tin of anchovies

zest and juice of 2 lemons

4 garlic cloves, finely chopped

1 handful of flat leaf parsley,
    finely chopped

3 tbsp capers, finely chopped

a dash of vegetable oil

sea salt and freshly ground
    black pepper

1 roll butcher's twine

This is the ultimate Sunday lunch dish: cost-effective, delicious and the oven does most of the work for you. Perfect with a mountain of Polenta roast potatoes (page 10) topped with butter, and a simple salad.

1 Preheat the oven to 150°C.

2 Lay the pork belly out on a chopping board skin-side up. Carefully remove 25% of the skin from the right-hand side of the belly by running your knife underneath (or you can ask your butcher to do this for you).

3 Using a small, sharp knife, cut some lines diagonally across the skin, just deep enough to reach the fat layer.

4 Now flip the belly over to the flesh side to begin seasoning by brushing the meat with the mustard. Next, season generously with salt and pepper before draping the anchovies all over the meat. Spread evenly with the lemon zest and garlic, then finally the parsley and capers.

5 Now roll the meat into a tube shape, like you would a Swiss roll. The skin needs to be on the outside, with the seasonings in the centre. Use the butcher's twine to tie and hold it together; I usually add about 8 single circles tied like shoelaces.

6 Once you have your roll, drizzle the skin with vegetable oil and sprinkle generously with more sea salt.

7 Place on a rack in the oven and cook for 3½ hours. Increase the oven temperature to 240°C for a further 20–30 minutes until the skin turns into crackling. For extra crispiness, you can also fry it in a smoking hot pan.

8 Allow the meat to rest for 10 minutes before removing the twine. Slice and serve.

Lamb shank hot pot

Serves 4

4 lamb shanks, cleaned

3 tbsp vegetable oil

3 onions, roughly chopped

4 carrots, roughly chopped

I celery stick, roughly chopped

I tbsp tomato paste

60g butter

6 tbsp plain flour

2 tbsp dried thyme

300ml red wine

800ml beef stock

3 tbsp Worcestershire sauce

3 tbsp soy sauce

100g frozen peas

8 large floury potatoes, such as
   Rooster, peeled and sliced about
   Icm thick

50g butter, melted

sea salt and freshly ground
   black pepper

This is a bit of a showstopper when it comes to impressing a crowd. Shanks provide a beautiful, almost gelatinous texture that's packed with flavour. Spend a bit of time braising them down and you will be handsomely rewarded with flavour. I've spent an extra few minutes fanning the potatoes on top with the shank bone so it looks the part: not essential, but what else would you be doing?

1 Preheat the oven to 150°C.
2 Place a large, heavy-based saucepan on a high heat. Add the lamb shanks and brown on all sides, getting as much colour as possible. Remove the shanks from the pan and set aside. Clean the fat from the pan and replace with 3 tablespoons of vegetable oil.
3 Add the vegetables and allow to caramelise all over. This should take about 10 minutes.
4 Now stir in the tomato paste, butter, flour and thyme and cook for a further minute until the flour is bubbling.
5 Add the red wine and simmer until reduced by half, then add the stock, Worcestershire sauce and soy sauce, then season with salt and pepper.
6 Return the shanks and their resting juices to the pan, then bring to the boil before covering with a lid and placing in the oven. Cook for 2–2½ hours, or until the shanks are soft to touch with the meat falling off the bone.
7 Remove the pot and increase the oven temperature to 200°C.
8 Using a fork, shred the meat off the shanks, being careful to discard any sinew or knuckle. Return the meat to the sauce and mix, then fold in the frozen peas. Retain one bone for some fancy design at the end!
9 Begin to layer the potatoes in a fan shape across the top of the lamb, placing a cleaned bone sticking out from the middle of the pot.
10 Brush the top with melted butter, season with salt, and bake for 45 minutes until the potatoes are golden brown and soft throughout.
11 As the hot pot rests, brush with more brown butter and some fresh thyme leaves. Serve to share in the middle of the table.

Slow-cooked lamb curry

2 tbsp olive oil

1kg bone-out leg or shoulder of
  lamb, diced (ask your butcher
  to do this if you like)

2 tbsp ground coriander

2 tbsp curry powder

2 tbsp ground cumin

1 tbsp chilli powder

4 onions

8 garlic cloves

2 red chillis, top removed (use
  dried if fresh are unavailable)

2 red peppers, seeds removed

2 tbsp Dijon mustard

2 chicken stock cubes

200ml red wine vinegar

2 x 400g tins of chopped
  tomatoes

1 beef stockpot

1 sprig of rosemary

salt and freshly ground
  black pepper

1 handful of coriander leaves,
  to garnish

Perfectly cooked rice (page 15),
  to serve

This is basically the style of lamb curry you'll get in the more authentic Indian take-aways, with that deep colour and chunky consistency. Now I won't attempt to claim its authenticity or regionality as I've never been to the country. However, I can promise it's packed with flavour, goes a long way, and uses up lots of bits from the vegetable tray in the fridge. You can mix and match some spices if you want and go a little heavier with the chilli for some extra fire.

1 Preheat the oven to 150°C.

2 Heat the oil in a large, flameproof casserole over a medium heat, add the lamb and fry, turning gently, for 2 minutes until caramelised all over.

3 In a separate non-stick pan, toast the spices over a medium heat for 1 minute until they become fragrant, then add them to the browned lamb.

4 In a food processer or blender, put the onions, garlic, chillis, peppers, mustard and stock cubes. Blend to a rough paste, then stir this into the browned lamb.

5 Continue to cook the mix over a medium heat for 3 minutes, stirring, then add the vinegar and allow to cook out for 30 seconds. Add the tinned tomatoes and stockpot. Add the rosemary and bring to the boil.

6 Place a lid on the dish and simmer very gently over a low heat for 3 hours until the meat is tender and the sauce is thick. Discard the rosemary. Adjust the seasoning with salt and pepper, if required, and serve with steamed rice.

Slow-roast lamb shoulder with Greek salad

1 whole lamb shoulder
  (about 1.5kg)
2 tbsp olive oil
3 garlic cloves
1 lemon, zest sliced off in 4 pieces,
  plus extra for seasoning

For the salad
20 cherry tomatoes, halved
1 cucumber, thinly sliced
100g feta, cubed
1 red onion, thinly sliced

For the dressing
5 tbsp olive oil
1 tbsp dried oregano
1 tbsp Dijon mustard
1 tbsp red wine vinegar
sea salt
juice of 1 lemon

Lamb and Greek salad are meant to be together. Try to get those beautifully ripe, sweet tomatoes for the salad and then just revel in that mixture of crispy lamb skin, rendered fat, soft meat, feta, herbs, onion … I could go on and on. Serve it with flatbreads (see page 56) and it is even better.

1 Preheat the oven to 150°C.
2 Spread some kitchen foil on a work surface, lay the whole shoulder on top, sprinkle with salt and olive oil. Stick a knife in the shoulder to create 8 holes, then fill these holes with 4 garlic cloves and 4 slices of lemon zest.
3 Wrap the kitchen foil into a parcel and place on a tray in the oven. Cook for 3 hours. Depending on your daily schedule, use the following timings: 150°C for 3 hours, 130°C for 5 hours, 110°C for 7 hours or 200°C for 1½ hours.
4 Pump the heat up to 220°C for the last 15–20 minutes of each timing and remove the top of the kitchen foil to caramelise the meat and crisp up the skin.
5 Remove the lamb shoulder from the oven and pull away the meat from the bone using a fork. Season the meat with some salt and lemon juice and zest.
6 To make the salad, put the tomatoes, cucumber and feta in a bowl. Add the red onion.
7 To make the dressing, whisk together the oil, vinegar, mustard and oregano before seasoning with salt and lemon juice.
8 Dress the salad lightly and serve alongside the lamb.

Irish stew

I whole lamb shoulder (1.5–2kg)

3 carrots

2 brown onions

2 leeks

2 tbsp vegetable oil

1.5 litres brown chicken stock

I handful of thyme

2 bay leaves

3 tbsp Worcestershire sauce

12 small new potatoes, peeled

100g pearl barley

I large handful of flat leaf parsley,
    chopped

sea salt and freshly ground
    black pepper

Nobody knows what the classic Irish stew should contain, and it's often a source of heated debate. Who knows? Anyway, for what it's worth, here's my version using diced lamb shoulder. It's the pearls of roasted lamb fat suspended in the broth that make Irish stew special for me.

1   Begin by preparing the lamb shoulder. Carefully remove the meat from the bone before cutting it into thumb-sized chunks. Don't worry if there is fat included as this adds to the flavour (or you can ask your butcher to do this for you). Retain the bone for the broth.

2   Peel the carrots and onions and wash the leeks. Cut the carrots into thumb-sized chunks, the onion into quarters and the leeks into thumb-sized chunks.

3   Place a large flameproof casserole dish over a high heat and add the oil. Season the lamb pieces with salt, add to the dish and fry for about 3 minutes to caramelise on all sides. Add the onions and fry for a few minutes to brown slightly to bring out the sweetness.

4   Now add the stock and bring to the boil, scraping the caramelised bits off the bottom with a wooden spoon to deglaze the pan.

5   Add the raw lamb bones from the shoulder, the carrots and leeks along with the thyme and bay leaves and bring the stock to the boil.

6   Season the broth with Worcestershire sauce, salt and black pepper before reducing the heat to a simmer. Cover the pot with a lid and cook over a very low heat for 3 hours until the lamb is soft.

7   Add the potatoes and pearl barley for the last 30 minutes so they cook through in the broth.

8   To finish, adjust the seasoning again and add all the chopped parsley before serving in warm bowls.

Beef Wellington

1kg beef fillet, trimmed with sinew
   removed (ask your butcher to
   prepare this)
2 tbsp vegetable oil
30 button mushrooms, blitzed to a
   fine crumb in a food processor
100g sheet of ready-made puff
   pastry
sea salt and freshly ground
   black pepper
a squeeze of lemon juice
3 sandwich wraps
egg yolks, for brushing

The story goes that it was named in honour of the
1st Duke of Wellington. This is a special-occasion
dish, no doubt. I've treated the recipe as if building
something, with very exact instructions. Nail each
stage and you will end up with a restaurant-quality
dish. I try to make this dish over two days; the fridge
time is key to allowing the rolls to set, giving you
a sharper finish and less stress. Patience is a key
ingredient.

1 Place a pan on a high heat and wait until it is smoking hot.
   Add some oil, season the meat, then brown the beef fillet all
   over, as quickly as possible.
2 Cool, then chill in the fridge.
3 In a separate pan, heat the mushroom mix over a high heat
   and cook for 5–6 minutes until all the liquid has evaporated,
   stirring constantly. It is very important that the mix becomes
   as dry as possible.
4 Finish with salt, pepper and lemon juice. Cool, then chill in
   fridge.

Stage 1 of build
1 Roll a sheet of clingfilm on a work surface.
2 Place the sandwich wraps down first, overlapping.
3 Add the mushrooms and spread in an even layer, about 1cm
   thick. Don't spread to the edge of the wraps, leave about
   2.5cm around the edge.
4 Place the browned beef fillet in the middle.
5 Roll the sandwich wraps over everything, into a cylinder
   shape. Continue rolling the clingfilm around to tighten the
   roll into a sausage shape, twist both ends around and place in
   the fridge for 1 hour to set.

Stage 2 of build
1 Roll a sheet of clingfilm on a work surface.
2 Place a sheet of puff pastry on the clingfilm.
3 Remove the beef roll from its clingfilm – it will hold in a
   sausage shape – and place on the puff pastry. >

4 Brush the top of the puff pastry, which will be the inside next to the beef, with egg yolk; this will help the pastry stick to the beef roll.

5 Roll the puff pastry over the beef roll in the same way as before, making sure to tighten the ends and leave no holes. Roll the clingfilm around the beef to tighten and return to the fridge to set for 1 hour.

Stage 3 of build

1 Remove the pastry and beef roll from the clingfilm.

2 Brush all over with the egg yolk, then leave in the fridge for 10 minutes.

3 Brush a second layer with egg yolk and get ready to decorate.

4 Decorate the wellington using cutters or simply by scoring the pastry with a knife. It's now finally ready for the oven!

Cooking

1 Option 1: Remove the beef from the fridge 30 minutes before cooking. Bake at 200°C for 35 minutes, then rest for 15 minutes before carving.

2 Option 2: Remove the beef from the fridge 30 minutes before cooking. Place a probe into the centre of the beef, cook to a core temperature of 48°C, remove from the oven and allow to rest until the temperature reaches 54°C. Carve.

Midweek shepherd's pie

2 tbsp vegetable oil

400g stewing lamb, diced

400g lamb mince

2 onions, diced

3 garlic cloves, roughly sliced

2 carrots, diced

I sprig of rosemary

2 tbsp fennel seeds

I tbsp tomato paste

2 tbsp plain flour

300ml red wine

2 chicken stockpots

I litre hot water

8 tbsp Worcestershire sauce

200g frozen peas

I handful of parsley, chopped

sea salt and freshly ground
   black pepper

For the potatoes

rock salt

6 large baking potatoes, such as
   Rooster

I egg yolk

50g Parmesan, grated

Here I've gone half and half with lamb mince and diced stewing lamb. The stewing lamb brings it up a level and, as always, the key is to get as much colour as possible on the meat at the start. This is another good one to bulk up on and reheat for lunch the next day or even freeze down.

1. Preheat the oven to 200°C.
2. Start with the potatoes. Add some rock salt to a baking tray and place the potatoes on top. Bake for 50 minutes until the skin is crispy and the potatoes soft throughout.
3. Meanwhile, in a large, heavy-based saucepan, heat the oil, add the diced lamb and colour all over. Follow this with the lamb mince and colour for a further 5 minutes.
4. Remove the meat from the pan and add the onions, garlic and carrots. Brown for 2 minutes before returning the meat and resting juices to the pan.
5. Build the flavours by adding rosemary, fennel seeds, tomato paste, flour and salt. Stir together.
6. Add the red wine and scrape the bottom of the pan using a wooden spoon. Mix the stockpots, hot water and Worcestershire sauce, then add to the pan. Bring to the boil, place a lid on top and leave over a low heat for 1 hour until the diced lamb is softened.
7. When the potatoes are ready, make a mash by removing the pulp and pushing it through a ricer. If you don't have a ricer, mash vigorously with a potato masher to make it as smooth as possible. Stir in the egg yolks and Parmesan, then set aside at room temperature.
8. When the lamb is tender, adjust the seasoning with salt and pepper and fold in the peas and parsley. Pour into an ovenproof dish, top with the potato and return to the oven for 20 minutes until golden brown. Serve warm.

Beef cheek lasagne

4 beef cheeks

2 tbsp vegetable oil

4 carrots, diced

2 onions, diced

4 garlic cloves, sliced

I sprig of rosemary

50g Parmesan cheese, rind
   separated and cheese grated

2 tbsp tomato paste

I large glass of red wine

I rich beef stockpot

2 × 400g tins of chopped
   tomatoes

50g capers

I large handful of flat leaf parsley

I pack of dried lasagne sheets

For the cheese sauce

500ml milk

50g butter

50g plain flour

50g white Cheddar

I tbsp Dijon mustard

zest and juice of I lemon

sea salt and freshly ground
   black pepper

This is comfort food on steroids. Ask your butcher to remove any gristle from the cheeks (always be cheeky and ask them to weigh them after to save some cash!). Beware, this is mega rich so expect to have some leftovers.

1 Preheat the oven to 150°C.
2 Cut the beef cheeks into small golf-ball sized chunks.
3 Place a large, heavy-based, flameproof casserole dish on a high heat and add the oil.
4 Season the beef cheeks with salt and pepper, then brown the meat chunks, getting as much colour as possible on all sides. Once browned, remove and place on a plate.
5 Reduce the heat to medium and add the carrots and onions and fry for 3 minutes to brown on all sides, being careful not to burn anything.
6 Next, add the garlic, rosemary, Parmesan rind and tomato paste and mix for 30 seconds before returning the beef cheeks and resting juices to the pan.
7 Increase the heat, add the wine and simmer to reduce by half. Add the beef stockpot and tomatoes. Bring the liquid to the boil, then cover and put in the oven for 3 hours.
8 After 3 hours, remove the pot from the oven; the beef will be soft. Break up the meat using a potato masher so that it will absorb more sauce. Don't forget to remove the Parmesan rind. Season with black pepper, capers and chopped parsley. Reset the oven to 200°C.
9 To make the cheese sauce, warm the milk to just above hand temperature. In a separate pan, melt the butter, then stir in the flour. Whisk in the warm milk and allow it to boil and thicken. Remove from the heat and finish with the grated Parmesan and Cheddar, mustard, lemon juice and zest.
10 To assemble, fill the bottom of an ovenproof dish with lasagne sheets, then a layer of beef cheek, then the cheese sauce. Continue this until the dish is full before finishing with a final layer of lasagne sheets, sauce and some extra grated cheese.
11 Cook in the preheated oven for 40 minutes until golden brown on top.

Part Five: Side Dishes and Breads

I must admit that sometimes the most exciting part of a restaurant menu are the breads, the dips and the sides! I have yet to learn the art of restraint and am regularly left with a large flock of 'bits', as I like to call them, surrounding our main plates at the table. I consider this chapter my ultimate collection of 'bits' with plenty of bread recipes to mop up all the goodness!

Baba ganoush

4 large aubergines

I garlic clove, grated

I tbsp tahini paste

I tbsp crème fraîche

I tsp ground cumin

I tsp ground coriander

I tsp chilli powder

5 tbsp good-quality olive oil,
    plus extra for drizzling

sea salt

lime or lemon juice

Aubergines can be tricky to make exciting, however they're inexpensive and a great way of bulking up salads and platters. Baba ganoush is seen in many forms around the eastern Mediterranean and is delicious as a starter or dip with breads and crackers. A good-quality olive oil is key and the barbecue adds a layer of flavour the oven can't compete with.

1   Place the aubergines on a barbecue for 15–20 minutes until the skin is blistered and the interior is soft throughout. Alternatively, roast in a 200°C oven for 30 minutes until the same texture is achieved.

2   Remove the pulp from inside the skin, place in a bowl, cool, then chill.

3   Add the garlic, tahini paste, crème fraîche, cumin, coriander, chilli powder and oil to the aubergine and whisk until smooth. Adjust the seasoning with salt and lime juice and drizzle with a little more olive oil.

4   Serve as a garnish or dip with crackers or bread.

Potato gratin

8 large baking potatoes, such as
  Rooster, peeled and sliced about
  5mm thick

400ml double cream

400ml milk

I whole nutmeg

3 cloves of garlic, halved

2 tbsp sea salt

40g Parmesan, grated

These are special-occasion potatoes. By warming the potato slices up in the milk and cream first, they release their starch and create that velvety, luxurious sauce. Feel free to add some grated garlic for gratin dauphinoise; I've gone retro with grated nutmeg. Delicious.

I Preheat the oven to 180°C.

2 Place 100ml of water in a large saucepan and add the cream, milk, nutmeg, garlic and salt. The water will protect the cream from burning into the bottom of the pan.

3 Add the sliced potatoes and bring the mix slowly to the boil. The starch will be released from the potatoes and will begin to thicken the cream.

4 Transfer the potatoes and all the sauce into a baking dish. Cover with grated Parmesan and bake in the oven for 50 minutes until golden brown on top and soft throughout.

Lentil dahl

Serves 4

3 tbsp vegetable oil

8 cardamom pods

4 bay leaves

4 dried red chillis

I tbsp ground cumin

4 garlic cloves, sliced

I large thumb-sized piece of
    ginger root, grated

I onion, finely diced

4 large tomatoes, chopped

400g green lentils

I litre water

I tbsp Dijon mustard

I vegetable stockpot

100g butter

zest and juice of I lime

I handful of coriander leaves

I chilli, finely sliced

sea salt

A chef colleague from Birmingham used to make this for staff dinner, and it immediately went into the hall of fame for staff meals. Packed with flavour, wholesome and warming, what really makes it is all the butter stirred in at the end. Cardamom pods are key, and you can get them in most supermarkets.

1 Heat a heavy-based saucepan over a medium heat and add the oil.

2 Add the cardamom, bay leaves, chillis and cumin and cook for 1 minute until they release their oils and gain a bit of colour, but don't let the mixture get too hot.

3 Now add the garlic and ginger and cook for 1 minute until golden brown.

4 Then add the onion and cook until soft and caramelised. This will take about 3–4 minutes. Everything should be nice and dark and sticky at this point.

5 Add the tomatoes and cook until they break down. Use a wooden spoon to scrape any crispy bits from the base of the pan.

6 Now add the lentils, water, mustard and vegetable stockpot. Bring to the boil, then simmer over a very low heat for about 30–40 minutes until the lentils are softened and have soaked up all the flavours.

7 Finish by adjusting the seasoning with salt, butter and the juice and zest of lime. Garnish with coriander leaves and sliced chilli. This will keep in the fridge for a few days and can be frozen down.

Baked quinoa salad with pomegranate, yogurt, lime and mint

2 tbsp vegetable oil

1 onion, diced

1 red pepper, diced

250g quinoa

1 tbsp ground cumin

2 tbsp coriander seeds

1 tbsp dried chilli flakes

1 litre chicken or vegetable stock

50g feta

1 pomegranate, seeds removed

zest and juice of 1 lime

50g yogurt

50g toasted sunflower seeds

1 handful of mint

1 handful of dill

sea salt

I usually make this for a platter alongside some grilled or barbecued meats. It's also a handy one to have in the fridge to bulk up lunches or light dinners. You can even try it with a fried egg for brunch.

1 Preheat the oven to 200°C.

2 Heat a heavy-based, overproof pan with the oil over a medium heat, add the onion and pepper and fry for 3 minutes until soft.

3 Add the quinoa, season with salt, then add the cumin, coriander and chilli and cook for a further 1 minute.

4 Add the stock and bring to the boil, place a lid on the pot and cook for 30 minutes in the oven until all the liquid has evaporated and the quinoa is fluffy to touch and soft. Remove from the pot at this point and allow the quinoa to chill in the fridge.

5 Once cold, spoon the quinoa onto a large plate. Dress the salad with the feta, pomegranate seeds, lime zest and juice. Drizzle with yogurt, then sprinkle with sunflower seeds, mint leaves and dill.

Caesar salad

2 heads of cos lettuce

1 handful of bread croûtons

4 tbsp grated Parmesan, for
    dressing

For the dressing

1 egg yolk

1 tbsp white wine vinegar

50g tin of high-quality anchovies
    (I use Ortiz)

1 tbsp Dijon mustard

1 thumb-sized chunk of Parmesan,
    grated

1 tbsp Worcestershire sauce

300ml vegetable oil

sea salt and freshly ground
    black pepper

The Caesar salad was supposedly conceived by Caesar Cardini at his Tijuana hotel in Mexico in the late 1920s. Ever since, a variety of versions have appeared. The beauty of this salad is in its simplicity, the key for me being the quality of anchovies in the dressing, which can be made in bulk and kept for a few days in the fridge.

1 To make the Caesar dressing, place the egg yolk, vinegar, half the anchovies, mustard, Parmesan and Worcestershire sauce in a blender. Blend to a paste, then pour this into a clean bowl.

2 Using a whisk, slowly add the oil until a loose dressing is formed, whisking continuously. Adjust the seasoning with salt and pepper at this point – it needs to pack a punch.

3 Remove the stalks from the lettuce heads and pull apart the individual leaves. Coat the lettuce leaves in the dressing and finish with croûtons and black pepper. Place in a bowl and top with grated Parmesan and the remaining anchovy fillets.

Ham hock mac and cheese

Serves 4

2 ham hocks (about 600g) with
   bone in
1½ tbsp butter
1½ tbsp plain flour
750ml warm milk
100g white Cheddar
30g Parmesan, grated
1 tablespoon Dijon mustard
½ chicken stockpot
juice of ½ lemon
200g macaroni, par-boiled in
   salted water and drained
sea salt and freshly ground
   black pepper

A tried-and-tested recipe brought to the next level with slow-cooked, salty ham hock. The addition of Dijon mustard also gives it a kick and avoids the stodgy feeling this dish can often deliver.

1   Place a large pan of water on the heat, add the ham hocks and bring to the boil. Reduce the heat, cover with a lid and simmer gently for 2 hours. The meat should be soft and just falling off the bone. Strain the hocks and carefully remove the meat, leaving behind the sinew and skin. Chop into evenly sized chunks, about the size of a thumbnail.

2   Preheat the oven to 180°C.

3   Place a saucepan on a medium heat and melt the butter. Add the flour and cook for 1 minute, stirring, until blonde in colour and bubbling.

4   Add the warm milk, whisking constantly until thickened and bubbling. Remove from the heat and add the Cheddar and Parmesan, mix together until glossy and smooth.

5   Stir in the the diced ham hock meat, mustard, stockpot, lemon juice, salt and pepper. Fold the precooked macaroni through the mix before transferring to a shallow, ovenproof dish.

6   Cook in the oven for 40 minutes until golden brown on top and warm throughout.

Cheesy white soda loaf

500g plain white flour

1 tsp bicarbonate of soda

1 tsp salt

400ml buttermilk (if you can't get
   buttermilk, add 3 tbsp yogurt
   and 3 tbsp lemon juice to 300ml
   of milk)

4 tbsp olive oil

20g Parmesan, grated

50g red Cheddar, cut into small
   chunks

50g leftover roast vegetables,
   roughly chopped (carrot,
   squash, red pepper, parsnip)

1 handful of cooked spinach
   or kale

1 tsp chilli flakes

1 tsp salt

butter, to serve

This is a really simple, homely dish that many of us will have made at some point. The bread soda is activated by the acidic buttermilk, creating air which causes the bread to rise as it cooks. This is a great one for bulking up dishes, or even to go in a lunchbox. I use cheese and leftover veg here but you can use almost anything from the fridge if you follow the quantities – a real all-rounder!

1   Preheat the oven to 190°C. Place an ovenproof baking tray inside to heat up.
2   To make the bread dough, mix the plain flour, bicarbonate of soda and salt in a bowl, making sure the bicarbonate of soda is evenly distributed so the bread will rise evenly. Make a well in the centre.
3   Reserve about a tablespoon of buttermilk for glazing, then mix the remainder with the olive oil in a separate bowl. Pour the mixture into the well in the flour.
4   Get your hands in and bring the mixture together, working it until it just forms a wet dough, otherwise the finished product will be dense.
5   Add the Parmesan and Cheddar, vegetables and spinach. Fold through the mix until they're incorporated.
6   Place the mix on a floured piece of parchment paper and roughly shape into a circle by patting down the top of the dough. This doesn't have to be too exact.
7   Cut 4 small lines across the top of the dough to create 8 wedge shapes. Brush the wedge sections with a little extra buttermilk and sprinkle with chilli flakes and salt. Leave a gap where you cut the lines. Now carefully transfer the parchment paper to the preheated tray in the oven.
8   Bake for 30–35 minutes until the base sounds hollow when tapped.
9   Cool on a wire rack, then tear and share with lots of butter.

Brioche garlic bread

For the brioche dough

400g strong plain flour, plus extra
    for dusting

40g sugar

I tsp salt

2 tsp fast-action dried yeast
    (I sachet)

100ml milk

4 eggs

100g soft butter

a little oil, for greasing

For the butter

100g butter

6 garlic cloves, grated

20g Parmesan, grated

I handful of parsley, chopped

sea salt and freshly ground
    black pepper

For the glaze

I egg yolk

2 tbsp cream

a handful of chives, snipped

I won't lie, this recipe is complicated but, my goodness, is it delicious! Just plan your day around it as it will repay the time and effort. You can eat it by itself or serve it with practically any dish in this book.

1   Start by making the butter. Mix the butter in a bowl with the garlic, Parmesan, parsley, salt and pepper until it is nicely blended. Roll into small balls around the size of a €2 coin and chill in the fridge.

2   Now to make the dough, put the flour, sugar, salt and fast-action yeast in a mixer bowl with a dough hook. Mix together so the dry goods are all evenly distributed.

3   Warm the milk to just above hand temperature in a small saucepan, then add it to the dough. Mix this together for 3 seconds on medium speed.

4   Add the eggs one by one and mix on medium speed for 5 minutes until the dough starts to come together and hug the hook.

5   Add the butter and mix for a further 8 minutes until the dough is shiny and glossy and just falling away from the dough hook when you lift it up.

6   Place in a greased bowl and allow to prove for an hour to double in size, but ideally leave it overnight in the fridge to slow prove.

7   Roll the dough on a floured surface into a sausage shape and cut into 8 x 60g chunks.

8   Brush a large baking tray with softened butter to stop the bread from sticking and preheat the oven to 185°C.

9   To assemble the doughballs, stuff the dough with the butter balls and shape into smooth balls using a small amount of flour. Place these on the baking tray, don't worry about the gaps. Cover with a cloth and leave in a warm place for about 45 minutes to double in size.

10   Once they've risen, mix together the egg yolk and cream for the glaze and brush the top of the bread using a pastry brush.

11   Bake in the oven for 15 minutes until golden brown all over.

12   Finish by brushing with more butter and sprinkling with salt and chives. Serve warm.

Part Six: Desserts and Cakes

Sweet treats to finish. I absolutely love the classics, and most of these dishes have been around for ever but have stood the test of time for a reason. I've kept things as simple as possible with little need for fancy equipment or gadgets. Carefully weigh out your ingredients, stick to the steps and revel in the results. I hope these are recipes you can return to again and again.

Steamed sticky toffee pudding with clotted cream

200g medjool dates

2 vanilla pods, split in half and
  seeds scraped out

120g unsalted butter, softened,
  plus extra for greasing

150g dark muscovado sugar

170g plain flour

2 tsp bicarbonate of soda

1 tsp grated nutmeg

2 whole eggs

For the toffee sauce

100g caster sugar

400ml double cream

50g butter

juice of ½ lemon

To serve

1 vanilla pod, split in half and
  seeds removed

100g clotted cream

I love sticky toffee pudding, and it's surprisingly easy to make. Steaming the pudding results in a softer texture as opposed to the crispy, baked finish. Here, I've made one large pudding that can be portioned after cooking. I always add a touch of lemon juice to the caramel sauce to liven it up a bit; a touch of salt helps, too. Ice cream is more than acceptable on top, but there's something a little grander about our vanilla clotted cream!

1   Place the dates, vanilla seeds and empty pod in a small saucepan. Just cover with water and bring to the boil over a medium heat. Turn down the heat and simmer gently for 30 minutes until soft the whole way through. Remove the vanilla pod, then transfer the softened dates to a blender and blend to a smooth purée, or use a hand blender. Leave to chill in the fridge.

2   Put the butter and sugar in a mixing bowl and blend to a paste using a hand mixer. Add the flour, bicarbonate of soda and nutmeg, then work in the eggs and mix together into a thick batter.

3   Fold the date purée through the mixture until smooth, then chill in the fridge until cold.

4   Grease the inside of a non-stick, heatproof 700ml pudding bowl heavily with butter, or prepare individual pudding moulds in the same way.

5   Fill the mould with the batter until three-quarters full. Seal the bowl with a layer of clingfilm, followed by kitchen foil.

6   Place the bowl in a saucepan and fill the pan with boiling water to come halfway up the side of the bowl. Cover and simmer gently for 1 hour until a metal skewer comes out clean from the pudding. Remove the foil and clingfilm, cool, then chill in the fridge until cold. >

7   To make the sauce, place the sugar in a heavy-based pan over a low heat until melted. Increase the heat to medium and cook for about 2–3 minutes, without stirring, until it forms a golden-brown caramel. Watch it carefully as it will be very hot. Carefully add the cream – it may split – and cook over a medium heat, stirring, until you have a smooth sauce. Blend in the butter and season with lemon juice. Set aside for serving.

8   Mix the vanilla seeds with the clotted cream and set aside for serving.

9   When it comes to serving, reheat the pudding in a saucepan of boiling water for 20 minutes, or in the microwave for 2–3 minutes, until warm throughout (10 minutes and 1–2 minutes respectively for individual puddings). Remove from the bowl and portion. Serve in bowls with the warm sauce and clotted cream.

Pineapple tipsy cake

Makes 900g cake

1 pineapple
100g caster sugar
100g ground almonds
100g plain flour
1 heaped tsp baking powder
50g olive oil
50g butter, melted
2 eggs
zest and juice of 1 lime

For the syrup
100ml rum
50g caster sugar
½ tbsp vanilla extract

For the caramel sauce
50g light soft brown sugar
100ml double cream

For the icing
100g crème fraîche
2 tsp icing sugar, sifted
½ tbsp vanilla extract
zest and juice of 1 lime

This is one of the simplest cake mixes around. The olive oil goes really well with the tropical fruit flavours and adds another layer of flavour. If you want to make a larger cake, you can double up the recipe and use a round cake tin.

1   Preheat the oven to 190°C. Line a loaf tin with baking parchment.
2   Peel the pineapple and remove the stalk. Place on a hot, dry pan and blacken the outside. Place on a chopping board and slice the edges, cut into half-moon shapes about 2cm thick. They should be just wide enough to fill the centre of the loaf tin.
3   Line the bottom of the tin with the pineapple, layered over each other slightly.
4   Mix the sugar, ground almonds, flour and baking powder in a bowl. Mix the olive oil, butter and eggs to form a paste, then stir it into the mixture. Finish with the lime zest and juice, then pour into the loaf tin on top of the pineapple. Bake for 55 minutes until a skewer inserted in the centre comes out clean.
5   As the cake cools, heat the rum, sugar and vanilla into a syrup and pour over the cake, allow it to soak in the fridge overnight so it becomes really dense and moist.
6   To make the caramel sauce, heat the brown sugar until a dark caramel is formed, add the cream and bring to the boil. Keep warm.
7   To make the icing, mix the crème fraîche, icing sugar, vanilla, lime juice and zest and whisk until thick.
8   Turn the tipsy cake out onto a plate, pour over the caramel sauce and serve with the crème fraîche icing.

Chocolate soufflé in a mug

Makes 2 large soufflés

80g caster sugar, plus extra
    for dusting

200g dark chocolate

2 egg yolks

2 tsp cornflour

200g milk

6 egg whites

soft butter to grease the mug

cocoa powder, for dusting

I have shed many tears over dodgy soufflés in the restaurant kitchen, but the addition of cornflour to this recipe makes your life easier by stabilising the mix. If you follow the steps carefully, you can create a dessert worthy of any restaurant menu – all from the comfort of your favourite mug! The ideal size of the mug for this recipe is 200ml.

1 Preheat the oven to 180°C.
2 Start by brushing your ovenproof mugs with soft butter, making sure the brushstrokes are straight up, then dust with caster sugar and place in the fridge.
3 Melt the chocolate in a heatproof bowl over a pan of boiling water, or you can do this in the microwave.
4 In a separate bowl, whisk together the egg yolks and cornflour.
5 Warm the milk in a small saucepan, then pour it on top of the egg/cornflour mix before whisking. Return this to the saucepan and cook over a low–medium heat, whisking until it forms a thick, smooth paste. It should bubble and turn glossy.
6 Add the paste to the melted chocolate and mix together; this is the base of the soufflé.
7 Whisk the egg whites at full speed using a hand blender until they form soft peaks. Add the sugar in 3 stages until the mixture forms stiff peaks.
8 Fold both mixes together carefully, making sure you do not knock out too much air.
9 Spoon the mix into the 2 mugs, tap on a work surface to remove any air bubbles and scrape away any excess mix with the back of a knife so you have an even surface. Run your thumb around the rim to clean it, then place on a flat tray in the oven.
10 Cook for 15 minutes until the soufflé has risen evenly and is flat on top.
11 When the soufflé is ready, remove carefully from the oven, dust with cocoa powder and serve warm.

Baileys bread and butter pudding

Serves 4

100g soft butter

10–12 slices white sliced bread

50g dried fruit, such as raisins,
	sultanas

50g dark chocolate chips

2 eggs

3 egg yolks

60g icing sugar, sifted

2 vanilla pods, seeds scraped out

300ml Baileys Irish cream liqueur

300ml single cream

4 tbsp light soft brown sugar

vanilla ice cream or custard,
	to serve

Like many great dishes, the origin of this dessert comes from making the most of leftover ingredients; in this case stale bread. It's great for using up store cupboard staples and can be made in advance – it's actually best reheated in the microwave. The Baileys adds another layer of comfort but you can leave it out if cooking for kids ... but it's miles better with Baileys.

1   Preheat the oven to 185°C.

2   Remove the crusts from the bread and spread the soft butter all over, then cut the bread into triangles. Use the remaining butter to grease an ovenproof baking tray.

3   Begin layering the bread triangles across the base of the dish, sprinkle a layer of dried fruit and chocolate chips on top, continue this process until all the bread is used and the tray is full.

4   In a separate bowl, whisk together the egg, egg yolks and icing sugar.

5   Put the vanilla seeds in a pan with the Baileys and cream and warm to just above hand temperature. Pour over the egg mix and whisk together until smooth, then then pour this over the layered bread in the tray.

6   Leave to rest at room temperature for 30 minutes, then sprinkle the top with brown sugar. Bake for 45 minutes until it has risen and wobbles.

7   Allow to rest for 30 minutes and then serve warm alongside vanilla ice cream or custard.

8   It can also last for a few days in the fridge.

Crème caramel

50g caster sugar

20ml water

2 large eggs

I egg yolk

20g caster sugar

250ml milk

20ml double cream

3 tsp vanilla extract

low-fat oil spray

More elegance in simplicity. This dish uses very few ingredients and is simpler to prepare than it appears. A great dinner party dessert and a velvety joy to eat when cooked perfectly.

I Preheat the oven to 100°C. Warm 2 medium-sized ramekins in the low oven, then remove and spray generously with a low-fat oil spray or brush with some vegetable oil.

2 Melt the sugar and water in a pan and bring to the boil, swirling the pan regularly. Do not mix with a spoon as it will be impossible to clean. Once the mix turns amber, remove from the heat and wait 1 minute until it's mahogany in colour.

3 Pour a thin layer of the caramel into the bottom of each ramekin and leave to cool at room temperature for 5 minutes.

4 Mix the eggs, egg yolk and caster sugar until smooth.

5 Warm the milk, cream and vanilla extract until just above hand temperature, pour over the eggs and mix until smooth, but be careful not to overwhisk or create too much air.

6 Pour the custard mix into the ramekins on top of the now-hardened caramel. Be generous, it should fill 90% of the ramekin.

7 Place in an ovenproof dish with some boiling water around the ramekins. Cover in clingfilm and cook in the oven for 45–50 minutes until the custards are set with a tiny amount of wobble. Remove and allow to return to room temperature.

8 Place in the fridge, ideally overnight, or for at least 4 hours, to allow the caramel layer to soften into the cream layer.

9 Release with a warm knife around the edges and turn out onto a plate to serve.

Tiramisu

Serves 6

450g mascarpone
3 eggs, separated
140g caster sugar
a pinch of sea salt
400ml espresso coffee
200ml brandy or amaretto
400g dried sponge fingers
50g dark cocoa powder

I won't lay claim to this recipe – I robbed it off a chef friend from just outside Milan. It's simple, it's a crowd pleaser and the quality really depends on the strength and level of the coffee you use. Tiramisu should be full of powerful flavours for me.

1   Take the mascarpone out of the fridge an hour in advance to soften.
2   Put the egg yolks in a mixer and whisk with 100g of the sugar until doubled in size and pale yellow in colour.
3   Fold this into the mascarpone and mix lightly until smooth.
4   Clean the mixer and add the egg whites, whisk with the remaining sugar until a meringue is formed, fold this into the mascarpone mix and set aside at room temperature, adding a pinch of sea salt to make it taste richer and creamier.
5   Warm the coffee with the alcohol and pour into a bowl. Begin assembling the tiramisu: Dip the sponge fingers in the coffee for 5 seconds to absorb the liquid, then layer them in the base of the tray.
6   Add an even layer of the cream and spread to fill the gaps. Repeat the process until the tray is full. Leave to set in the fridge for 3 hours or overnight if possible.
7   Remove the tiramisu from the cake tin, dust the top with cocoa powder, cut into squares and serve.

Panna cotta with almonds and raspberries

600ml double cream

400ml milk

120g icing sugar, sifted

3 vanilla pods, seeds scraped out

4 gelatine leaves

5 tbsp flaked almonds

50g ripe raspberries

a little vegetable oil, for greasing

a few mint leaves, to garnish

Panna cotta is a classy dessert relying on quality milk and just the right amount of gelatine to achieve that signature wobble. Gelatine leaves are available in most supermarkets and are very handy for restaurant-style dessert-making. Toasted almonds and ripe raspberries are the perfect garnish, but any seasonal berries will do.

1 Place six ramekins or mini pudding moulds on a tray and brush lightly with some vegetable oil.

2 Place the cream, milk, icing sugar and vanilla seeds and pods in a saucepan and warm gently over a low heat without allowing the mixture to boil.

3 Place the gelatine leaves in a bowl of cold water until they soften.

4 Once the sugar has dissolved in the milk and cream, remove it from the heat and pour the mix into a jug through a fine sieve. Strain the gelatine and stir into the milk and cream until dissolved.

5 Leave the mixture at room temperature for an hour to cool, then stir again before pouring the mix into the pre-oiled moulds.

6 Chill in the fridge until set, cold and wobbly to touch.

7 Place the almonds in a preheated oven at 150°C for 10 minutes until golden brown all over.

8 To serve, dip the panna cotta moulds in some boiling water before turning out onto a plate; they should wobble but hold their shape. Garnish with the raspberries, almonds and some mint leaves and serve.

Chocolate fondant with custard

110g butter

110g dark chocolate with
   70% cocoa solids

2 egg yolks

2 eggs

110g caster sugar

110g plain flour

For the fondant filling

100g dark chocolate with 70%
   cocoa solids, broken into pieces

150ml single cream

For the custard

4 egg yolks

60g caster sugar

2 vanilla pods, seeds scraped out

250ml single cream

For dusting

2 tbsp caster sugar, for lining
   the moulds

2 tbsp cocoa powder, for dusting
   the finished fondant

Hard to ignore a dessert menu when there's a chocolate fondant on it. I've cheated slightly by creating a chocolate ganache ball to fill your fondant with, meaning you'll be guaranteed a liquid centre every time.

1 Preheat the oven to 180°C. Brush some ramekins or small pudding moulds with a small amount of softened butter before dusting with caster sugar.

2 To make the fondant filling, put the chocolate pieces in a bowl. Bring the cream to the boil in a small pan, then pour over the chocolate and mix until smooth. Chill in fridge.

3 To make the custard, place the egg yolks, sugar and vanilla seeds in a bowl and mix together to form a paste.

4 Heat the cream in a saucepan until almost boiling, then pour into the egg mix and stir together.

5 Return the liquid to the pan and cook slowly over a low heat, mixing constantly with a spatula until the cream thickens. Don't overcook or it will turn to scrambled eggs. Pour into a bowl, cover with clingfilm and cool in the fridge.

6 To make the fondant mix, melt the butter and chocolate over a heatproof bowl set over a pan of gently simmering water or even in the microwave.

7 In a separate bowl, whisk the egg yolks, eggs and sugar using a hand blender until a light, airy mix has formed. It should double in size.

8 Fold the flour into the eggs, then stir in the melted chocolate and butter. Pour this mix into the sugar-lined ramekins or moulds to fill two-thirds of the way up.

9 Scoop out some of the firm chocolate fondant filling from the fridge and roll into a small ball in your hand, just smaller than a €2 coin. Make 6 balls. Press one into each of the fondants, then cover the holes with a small amount of mix to hide the balls.

10 Bake for 10 minutes. Turn out onto serving plates. Mix the sugar and cocoa and use to dust the fondants. Serve immediately with the cold custard.

Monica's meringue roulade

Serves 8

6 egg whites

300g caster sugar

2 tsp malt vinegar

2 tsp cornflour

2 tsp vanilla extract

300ml double cream, whipped

50g ripe raspberries

a little icing sugar, sifted,
   for dusting

Monica is my mum, and this is her signature dish. It's worthy of any restaurant menu in my opinion and even with all my so-called training, it doesn't taste the same when I make it! The key moments include the cornflour in the meringue and covering with a cloth as it cools to keep it pliable for rolling. I hope you enjoy this as much as our family has through the years.

1 Preheat the oven to 150°C and line a 35×27cm baking tray with parchment paper.

2 Whisk the egg whites using a hand mixer until it forms soft peaks. Add one-third of the sugar then continue to whisk before adding the remaining sugar and whisking until you have a thick, glossy meringue.

3 Mix the vinegar, cornflour and vanilla extract into a paste and whisk this through the meringue for another minute.

4 Spread the meringue evenly across the parchment paper, about 2.5cm thick.

5 Bake in the oven for 15 minutes, then remove and cover with a cloth until cooled.

6 Dust a separate sheet of baking parchment with some icing sugar and carefully turn the meringue sheet onto it.

7 Line the inside of the sheet with whipped cream and fruit, leaving a thumb-sized gap around the edges.

8 Using the baking parchment as support, roll the meringue over itself to create a cylinder. Dust with some more icing sugar before slicing and sharing.

Bakewell tart

Serves 8

For the pastry

450g plain flour, plus extra
    for dusting
150g icing sugar, sifted, plus
    extra for dusting
1 pinch of salt
220g soft butter
2 eggs
1 egg, for glazing

For the tart filling

5 tbsp high-quality raspberry jam
270g soft butter
270g caster sugar
270g ground almonds
2 tbsp plain flour
2 whole eggs
1 egg yolk (from the pastry)
2 vanilla pods, seeds scraped out
2 tbsp brandy
20g flaked almonds

As a kid, I used to go to the shop and buy the cheap packet of six Mr Kipling bakewell tarts, often eating them in one sitting! Here is a slightly classier version lined with raspberry jam and a frangipane filling, to give it its technical term. You can buy a quality tart case to use instead of making your own.

1   Mix the flour, icing sugar and salt together in a mixer. Add the soft butter and mix to a crumb. Bind with the 2 eggs, then wrap in clingfilm and rest overnight in the fridge.

2   Roll out the pastry on a lightly floured work surface to about 2.5cm thick, cut into a circle and chill in the fridge.

3   Use the pastry to carefully line a tart case, allowing some overhang, then chill in fridge.

4   Preheat the oven to 170°C.

5   Cover the pastry with a piece of baking parchment, then fill with baking beans. Bake the tart case blind for 15 minutes, then carefully remove the beans and paper and return to the over for a further 15–20 minutes until golden brown.

6   Separate the remaining egg and put the yolk aside for the filling. Brush the case with the egg white from the extra egg, then return it to the oven for 2 minutes to glaze.

7   Using a grater, gently file back the excess pastry until you reach the edge of the tart ring.

8   Raise the oven temperature to 190°C.

9   Spread the jam evenly across the base of the tart case, stopping just short of the edge.

10 In a mixer, blend the butter and caster sugar for 1 minute until it turns pale in colour. Add the ground almonds, flour, eggs and remaining egg yolk and mix lightly until it just comes together. Finish the filling with the seeds from the vanilla pods and the brandy.

11 Pour the mixture into the tart case on top of the jam. It should fill 80% of the tart case, allowing it to rise to the rim during cooking.

12 Decorate the top with the flaked almonds and cook for 30–35 minutes until a skewer inserted in the centre comes away clean. Remove and allow to come to room temperature, dust ever so lightly with icing sugar and serve.

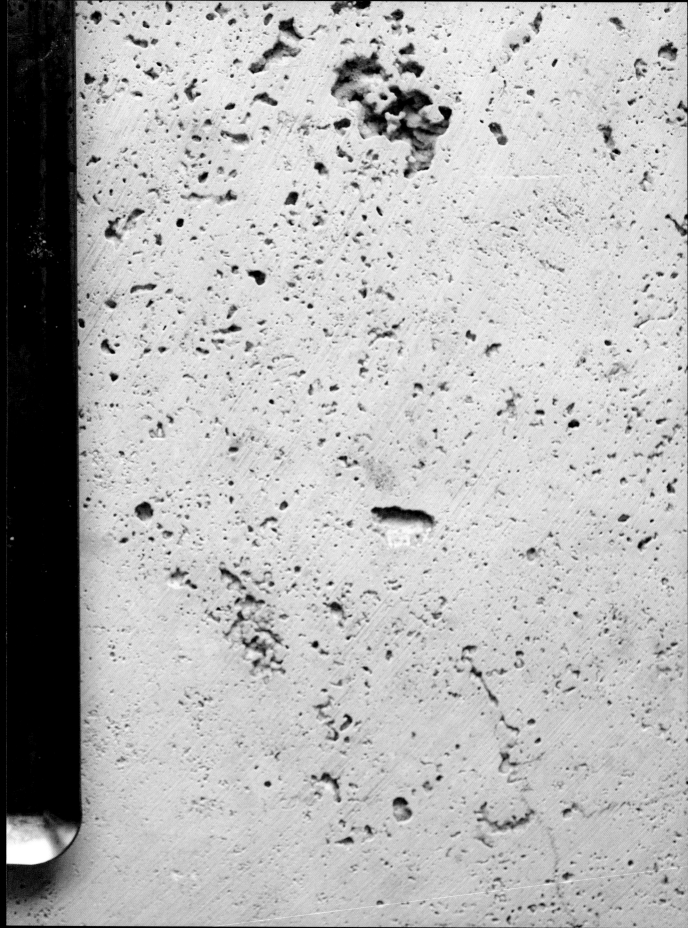

Custard tart

Serves 8

For the pastry

450g plain flour, plus extra
 for dusting

150g icing sugar, sifted

1 pinch of salt

220g soft butter

2 eggs

For the filling

1 litre single cream

12 egg yolks

200g icing sugar, sifted

4 tbsp Cognac

1 whole nutmeg

This might appear a little bit technical but the results are magic. If you want to avoid the stress of making a tart case, you can buy a quality shop-bought version. The filling is very simple to make and when cooked properly and served with that slight wobble, this dessert is hard to beat.

1 To make the pastry, mix together the flour, icing sugar and salt in a mixer, using the paddle attachment. Add the soft butter and mix until it looks like fine breadcrumbs.

2 Add the eggs and mix together at a high speed for 30 seconds until it becomes a paste. Wrap in clingfilm and chill overnight in the fridge.

3 Preheat the oven to 170°C.

4 Roll out the pastry on a lightly floured work surface to about 1cm thick. Chill in the fridge again for 5 minutes to firm it up.

5 Now, carefully line a tart case with the pastry, allowing some overhang, then chill in the fridge for 5 minutes.

6 Cover the pastry with a piece of baking parchment, then fill with baking beans. Bake the tart case blind for 15 minutes, then carefully remove the beans and paper and return the case to the oven for a further 15–20 minutes until golden brown.

7 To make it really neat and tidy, gently file back the excess pastry using a fine grater until you reach the edge of the tart ring. The case is now ready for the filling.

8 Reduce the oven temperature to 110°C.

9 To make the filling, put the cream in a saucepan and simmer over a low heat for 5 minutes to warm.

10 Mix the egg yolks, icing sugar and Cognac together until smooth. Strain the warm cream through a sieve over this mix and stir gently with a wooden spoon.

11 Place the tart case on a tray in the oven. Carefully pour the mix into it, trying to avoid creating air bubbles. Use a cocktail stick to remove any that form. Cook for 50–60 minutes until the custard is completely set in the middle.

12 Remove from the oven and allow to sit at room temperature for at least 2 hours. Grate some fresh nutmeg over the top before slicing and serving.

Eton mess with strawberries and basil

700ml double cream

4 egg yolks

2 vanilla pods, seeds scraped out

80g icing sugar, sifted, plus extra
  for the coulis

100g ripe strawberries

4 premade meringue nests,
  lightly crushed

a few small basil leaves, to garnish

A simple dessert and a great way to showcase quality fruit. The mixture of the custard and whipped cream pulls this dessert up from the average category, especially with the vanilla pod. Basil and strawberry go wonderfully together and the better the fruit, the better this dish will eat. It looks pretty fancy as well!

1 Place 500ml of the cream in a saucepan and bring to the boil.
2 While it's boiling, place the egg yolks, vanilla seeds and pods and icing sugar in a bowl and mix. Once the liquid has boiled, pour the warm cream on top and mix. Then return the mixture to the pan and cook over a medium heat, stirring constantly, until the cream begins to thicken and coats the back of a spoon. Remove from the heat and leave to cool slightly, then chill in the fridge. Remove the vanilla pods.
3 When the custard is cold, lightly whip the remaining 200ml of cream and fold through the custard. Whisk again until thick and holding stiff peaks.
4 To make the coulis, place one-third of the strawberries in a blender with a little icing sugar to taste and blend to a sauce consistency. Cut the rest of the strawberries into chunks.
5 Assemble the dessert in cocktail glasses, adding layers of vanilla cream, coulis, crushed meringue and strawberries until the glasses are full. Finish with crushed meringue and some small basil leaves.

Apple tart

I large sheet of frozen puff pastry

70g soft butter

70g caster sugar

70g ground almonds

I tbsp plain flour

½ egg, lightly whisked

I tsp vanilla extract

2 tbsp brandy

8 green eating apples, such as
Granny Smith

20g icing sugar, sifted

3 tbsp apricot jam

vanilla ice cream, to serve

We used to use the pastry trimmings and apple scraps in the restaurant kitchen to make this dish. It put a smile on the troops' faces with a cup of coffee just before service would begin – the small wins! The key to a crispy tart base is cooking on a preheated tray in the oven.

1 Preheat the oven to 210°C, placing a heavy baking tray in the oven.
2 Cut the pastry into a rectangle shape and place on a sheet of baking parchment. Make sure there is plenty of parchment to catch excess sugar later.
3 To make the almond paste, whip the butter and sugar together in a bowl. Fold in the almonds, flour and egg. Bring this together using a whisk and finish by adding the vanilla and brandy.
4 Peel the skin from the apples and cut out the core. Using a knife, slice the apple halves horizontally about 5mm thick.
5 To assemble the tart, pierce the pastry using a fork to prevent it from rising, but leave the outer rim alone so this rises during cooking.
6 Spread a thin, even layer of the almond paste on the area of the pastry with the fork holes, then layer your apple slices in a fan pattern along the pastry.
7 Once complete, dust the icing sugar all over the tart using a sieve. Use the baking parchment to carefully lift the tart onto the preheated baking tray in the oven.
8 Cook for 20–25 minutes until it is dark golden brown and the pastry has risen around the edges.
9 Melt the apricot jam in a pan with about 1 tablespoon of water and brush this on top of the apples to create a shine. Serve the slices warm with vanilla ice cream.

No-churn vanilla ice cream

1 litre double cream
350g caster sugar
100ml water
8 egg yolks
2 vanilla pods, seeds scraped out

This recipe was kindly handed down to me from my first head chef, Noel (thanks for putting up with me, Noel). It makes perfect soft-set vanilla ice cream without the need for any fancy equipment or machines. It goes really well with many of the desserts in this book, so I always have some stored in lunchboxes in the freezer.

1   For the first stage, place the cream in a large bowl and whisk until it holds stiff peaks. Keep it in the fridge until needed.
2   Next, put the caster sugar and the water in a saucepan and bring to the boil, then continue to boil for 1 minute to thicken slightly into a syrup.
3   Set up a mixer with the whisk attachment. Whisk the egg yolks and vanilla seeds at a high speed until they begin to turn pale in colour and double in size.
4   Slowly add the sugar syrup to the egg mix in a constant stream until it is all incorporated. Continue whisking the mix until it doubles in size, turns white and thickens.
5   Fold this egg and sugar mix into the whipped cream until smooth. Pour into a container of your choice, cover with parchment and freeze overnight.
6   When ready to use, remove from the freezer and scoop using a spoon. It should be the texture of soft serve.

Pistachio and chocolate chip cookies

360g plain flour

1 heaped tsp baking powder

200g butter

200g caster sugar

170g light soft brown sugar

1 egg

1 egg yolk

200g dark chocolate with 70% cocoa solids, roughly chopped

100g roasted pistachios, roughly chopped

This is a great recipe for stocking up your freezer. You can have a batch of dough ready to go and pop them into the oven for your cup of tea in the evening.

1 If cooking straight away, preheat the oven to 170°C.

2 Mix the flour and baking powder in a bowl.

3 Place the butter, caster and brown sugar in a separate bowl and cream until light and smooth.

4 Now add the egg and egg yolks and mix together, then gently fold in the flour, followed by the chocolate and nuts. Chill in the fridge for an hour.

5 Next, roll the dough into small balls in your hands, just smaller than a golf ball. These can be cooked straight away or placed in a container and frozen.

6 To cook immediately, place well spaced out on a greased baking sheet and bake for 12 minutes. Leave to cool on the tray for 5 minutes, then transfer to a wire rack to cool.

7 To cook straight from the freezer, increase the cooking time to 18 minutes.

Marie's scones

450g self-raising flour, plus
  extra for dusting
60g caster sugar, plus extra
  for glazing
120g butter
240ml milk
3 eggs
raspberry jam, melted butter and
  whipped cream, to serve

Marie was the mum of one of my good friends and she made these scones every weekend. She would freeze them in batches to be microwaved back to life for breakfast. If I was staying over, I'd sneak down early and devour about five of them before anyone else woke up – they were that good. She's kindly donated the recipe and insists they are served with raspberry jam and melted butter.

1 Preheat the oven to 190°C and place a flat baking tray in the oven.
2 Place the flour and sugar in a bowl and mix. Now add the butter and rub with your hands until you have a crumb-like texture.
3 Warm the milk to hand temperature and add to the mix along with 2 of the eggs. Bring the mix together very gently until everything is just incorporated. If we overmix at this stage, the scone texture will become tough and dry.
4 Lightly dust a work surface with flour and roll out the dough on a lightly floured work surface into a rectangle about 5cm thick, making sure the dough is nice and smooth.
5 Beat the remaining egg and brush it over the dough, then dust evenly with caster sugar.
6 Using a smooth round cutter, cut the round scones sharply. Remove the excess dough.
7 Place a sheet of baking parchment on the preheated tray and transfer the scones. Bake for 12–15 minutes until slightly risen.
8 Serve with melted butter, jam and whipped cream.

Carrot loaf-tin cake

Makes 900g cake

2 eggs

125ml coconut oil

100g caster sugar

75g light soft brown sugar

140g plain flour

1 tsp baking powder

1 tsp salt

1 tsp grated nutmeg

1 tsp ground cinnamon

zest of ½ orange

3 carrots, finely grated and tops
    reserved

25g walnuts, toasted and chopped

25g dates, chopped

1 tsp vanilla extract

For the syrup

200ml fresh orange juice

100ml brandy

100g light soft brown sugar

For the icing

320g cream cheese

60g icing sugar, sifted

zest and juice of 1 lemon

Carrot cake and a cup of tea on a Sunday is right up there for me. No word of a lie, one of the best carrot cakes I've had was from a petrol station in the Irish countryside. I photographed the ingredients on the packaging and after a few attempts came up with the following recipe. The loaf tin is the perfect shape and size as well.

1   Preheat the oven to 180°C and line a 900g loaf tin with baking parchment.

2   In a mixing bowl, whisk to combine the eggs, oil, caster and brown sugar.

3   Now add the flour, baking powder, salt, spices and orange zest, stirring until you have a fairly wet batter.

4   Finish the batter by folding in the carrots, walnuts, dates and vanilla extract.

5   Pour into the prepared loaf tin and bake for 40 minutes until a skewer inserted in the centre comes out clean.

6   Turn the cake out of the tin, remove the baking parchment and place on a wire rack to cool. Slice in half horizontally using a serrated knife.

7   While the cake is cooling, place the orange juice, brandy and brown sugar in a pot and bring to the boil. Spoon some of the syrup over both slices until it soaks in.

8   To make the icing, whisk the cream cheese, icing sugar and lemon zest and juice in a bowl until smooth.

9   Spread a layer of the icing on one half of the cake, then sandwich the cake back together. Using a piping bag and nozzle, decorate the top of the cake with the remaining icing. Garnish with carrot tops and walnuts. Slice and serve.

Triple-chocolate brownies

275g dark chocolate with 70% cocoa solids

275g butter

325g caster sugar

4 large eggs, lightly beaten

175g plain flour

1 tsp baking powder

50g white chocolate, chopped into chunks

50g milk chocolate, chopped into chunks

The picture speaks a thousand words. These are indulgent and rich. The recipe is all about stage 6: cook just until the top is baked but the brownie remains soft and indulgent inside.

1 Preheat the oven to 180°C and line a shallow 20×30cm baking tin with greaseproof paper.

2 Put the dark chocolate and butter in a heatproof bowl and melt over a pan of gently simmering water. Add the sugar and stir until dissolved, then allow to cool slightly.

3 Fold the eggs into the mix.

4 Mix the flour and baking powder together so they are evenly distributed, then gradually fold in the flour mixture in three stages, being careful not to overmix.

5 Finish by folding in the chocolate chunks. Pour the mix into your prepared tin.

6 Bake for 20–25 minutes until the top is baked but the brownies remain soft inside. When it comes out of the oven it might look a little wobbly in the middle. This is good.

7 Allow to rest at room temperature before chilling in the fridge and cutting into portions. The brownies will keep in the fridge for a couple of days.

Acknowledgements

Firstly, I would like to acknowledge you, the reader, and thank you sincerely for reading or buying the book. It means a lot to put something out there in public, and hopefully have people take notice.

As a chef who cooks food for a living, the task of writing a book is a daunting one. It takes various skills and expertise that bear no resemblance to the skills needed in a professional kitchen day to day: patience, thoughtfulness, coherence and calm. For that, I'd like to thank Sarah and the team at Gill Books for guiding me through the process and allowing me to showcase my food so seamlessly.

To do that, we needed a fantastic team on the ground, capturing the dishes at their best and generally attempting to make me look good. (I hope it worked!) Thank you to Cliodhna Prendergast for the stunning imagery, Orla Neligan for your effortless style and patience, and John Donnelly for soldiering with me in the kitchen across some very long days. We were a small team, but it was so much fun to work alongside such passionate, hard-working and talented people. And the craic was good!

Massive thanks to Noel, Niamh, Andy and all the team at NK for keeping me on the straight and narrow for all these years. Looking forward to many more.

Thank you to Brian Walsh in RTÉ for taking a chance on a 26-year-old chancer. Looking forward to many more series. Thanks also to Marc, Robin and the teams past and present at Appetite Media for putting all our random ideas on screen so beautifully.

All these recipes come from years of learning from incredible chefs. I will always be indebted to the people who taught and cared for me while making working in a kitchen a complete joy. There are too many to note, but a special mention to the 'bosses': Noel, Chef Kevin, Sweeney, The Doc and, lastly, Mick.

Finally, I am extremely fortunate to have such a supportive family who have always encouraged me to try my best. Thanks to my parents, Monica and Tom (hopefully you're getting that payback for all those Tuesday-morning 5 a.m. lifts to Dawson St!), and my sister, Laura.

And, of course, much love to the real boss, Gráinne. I'd be lost without you.

Index